WILLIAM

The First Part of
the History of
Henry the Fourth

PENGUIN BOOKS

Penguin Books Ltd, Harmondsworth, Middlesex, England
Penguin Books Australia Ltd, Ringwood, Victoria, Australia

—

Published by Penguin Books 1938
Revised and enlarged 1955
Reprinted 1961, 1964, 1965, 1968

—

Made and printed in Great Britain
by Cox & Wyman Ltd,
London, Fakenham and Reading
Set in Monotype Bembo

The Editor gratefully acknowledges
the kindness of Dr J. C. Adams in
allowing the Penguin Shakespeare to
reproduce an engraving of his
model of the stage of the
Globe Playhouse

The portraits on the cover and on the title page
were engraved by Reynolds Stone

—

CONTENTS

THE WORKS OF SHAKESPEARE

APPROXIMATE DATE	PLAYS		FIRST PRINTED
Before 1594	HENRY VI *three parts*	*Folio*	1623
	RICHARD III		1597
	TITUS ANDRONICUS		1594
	LOVE'S LABOUR'S LOST		1598
	THE TWO GENTLEMEN OF VERONA		*Folio*
	THE COMEDY OF ERRORS		*Folio*
	THE TAMING OF THE SHREW		*Folio*
1594–1597	ROMEO AND JULIET (*pirated* 1597)		1599
	A MIDSUMMER NIGHT'S DREAM		1600
	RICHARD II		1597
	KING JOHN		*Folio*
	THE MERCHANT OF VENICE		1600
1597–1600	HENRY IV *part i*		1598
	HENRY IV *part ii*		1600
	HENRY V (*pirated* 1600)		*Folio*
	MUCH ADO ABOUT NOTHING		1600
	MERRY WIVES OF WINDSOR (*pirated* 1602)		*Folio*
	AS YOU LIKE IT		*Folio*
	JULIUS CAESAR		*Folio*
	TROYLUS AND CRESSIDA		1609
1601–1608	HAMLET (*pirated* 1603)		1604
	TWELFTH NIGHT		*Folio*
	MEASURE FOR MEASURE		*Folio*
	ALL'S WELL THAT ENDS WELL		*Folio*
	OTHELLO		1622
	LEAR		1608
	MACBETH		*Folio*
	TIMON OF ATHENS		*Folio*
	ANTONY AND CLEOPATRA		*Folio*
	CORIOLANUS		*Folio*
After 1608	PERICLES (*omitted from the Folio*)		1609
	CYMBELINE		*Folio*
	THE WINTER'S TALE		*Folio*
	THE TEMPEST		*Folio*
	HENRY VIII		*Folio*

POEMS

DATES UNKNOWN	VENUS AND ADONIS	1593
	THE RAPE OF LUCRECE	1594
	SONNETS } A LOVER'S COMPLAINT }	1609
	THE PHOENIX AND THE TURTLE	1601

WILLIAM SHAKESPEARE

William Shakespeare was born at Stratford upon Avon in April, 1564. He was the third child, and eldest son, of John Shakespeare and Mary Arden. His father was one of the most prosperous men of Stratford, who held in turn the chief offices in the town. His mother was of gentle birth, the daughter of Robert Arden of Wilmcote. In December, 1582, Shakespeare married Ann Hathaway, daughter of a farmer of Shottery, near Stratford; their first child Susanna was baptized on May 6, 1583, and twins, Hamnet and Judith, on February 22, 1585. Little is known of Shakespeare's early life; but it is unlikely that a writer who dramatized such an incomparable range and variety of human kinds and experiences should have spent his early manhood entirely in placid pursuits in a country town. There is one tradition, not universally accepted, that he fled from Stratford because he was in trouble for deer stealing, and had fallen foul of Sir Thomas Lucy, the local magnate; another that he was for some time a schoolmaster.

From 1592 onwards the records are much fuller. In March, 1592, the Lord Strange's players produced a new play at the Rose Theatre called *Harry the Sixth,* which was very successful, and was probably the *First Part of Henry VI.* In the autumn of 1592 Robert Greene, the best known of the professional writers, as he was dying wrote a letter to three fellow writers in which he warned them against the ingratitude of players in general, and in particular against an 'upstart crow' who 'supposes he is as much able to bombast out a blank verse as the best of you: and being an absolute Johannes Factotum is in his own conceit the only

Shake-scene in a country.' This is the first reference to Shakespeare, and the whole passage suggests that Shakespeare had become suddenly famous as a playwright. At this time Shakespeare was brought into touch with Edward Alleyne the great tragedian, and Christopher Marlowe, whose thundering parts of Tamburlaine, the Jew of Malta, and Dr Faustus Alleyne was acting, as well as Hieronimo, the hero of Kyd's *Spanish Tragedy*, the most famous of all Elizabethan plays.

In April, 1593, Shakespeare published his poem *Venus and Adonis*, which was dedicated to the young Earl of Southampton: it was a great and lasting success, and was reprinted nine times in the next few years. In May, 1594, his second poem, *The Rape of Lucrece*, was also dedicated to Southampton.

There was little playing in 1593, for the theatres were shut during a severe outbreak of the plague; but in the autumn of 1594, when the plague ceased, the playing companies were reorganized, and Shakespeare became a sharer in the Lord Chamberlain's company who went to play in the Theatre in Shoreditch. During these months Marlowe and Kyd had died. Shakespeare was thus for a time without a rival. He had already written the three parts of *Henry VI*, *Richard III*, *Titus Andronicus*, *The Two Gentlemen of Verona*, *Love's Labour's Lost*, *The Comedy of Errors*, and *The Taming of the Shrew*. Soon afterwards he wrote the first of his greater plays – *Romeo and Juliet* – and he followed this success in the next three years with *A Midsummer Night's Dream*, *Richard II*, and *The Merchant of Venice*. The two parts of *Henry IV*, introducing Falstaff, the most popular of all his comic characters, were written in 1597–8.

The company left the Theatre in 1597 owing to disputes over a renewal of the ground lease, and went to play at the

Curtain in the same neighbourhood. The disputes contin-
ued throughout 1598, and at Christmas the players settled
the matter by demolishing the old Theatre and re-erecting
a new playhouse on the South bank of the Thames, near
Southwark Cathedral. This playhouse was named the
Globe. The expenses of the new building were shared by
the chief members of the Company, including Shakespeare,
who was now a man of some means. In 1596 he had bought
New Place, a large house in the centre of Stratford, for £60,
and through his father purchased a coat-of-arms from the
Heralds, which was the official recognition that he and his
family were gentlefolk.

By the summer of 1598 Shakespeare was recognized as
the greatest of English dramatists. Booksellers were print-
ing his more popular plays, at times even in pirated or stolen
versions, and he received a remarkable tribute from a young
writer named Francis Meres, in his book *Palladis Tamia*. In
a long catalogue of English authors Meres gave Shakespeare
more prominence than any other writer, and mentioned by
name twelve of his plays.

Shortly before the Globe was opened, Shakespeare had
completed the cycle of plays dealing with the whole story
of the Wars of the Roses with *Henry V*. It was followed by
As You Like it, and *Julius Caesar,* the first of the maturer
tragedies. In the next three years he wrote *Troylus and
Cressida, The Merry Wives of Windsor, Hamlet,* and *Twelfth
Night.*

On March 24, 1603, Queen Elizabeth I died. The company
had often performed before her, but they found her suc-
cessor a far more enthusiastic patron. One of the first acts
of King James was to take over the company and to pro-
mote them to be his own servants, so that henceforward
they were known as the King's Men. They acted now very

frequently at Court, and prospered accordingly. In the early years of the reign Shakespeare wrote the more sombre comedies, *All's Well that Ends Well,* and *Measure for Measure,* which were followed by *Othello, Macbeth,* and *King Lear.* Then he returned to Roman themes with *Antony and Cleopatra* and *Coriolanus.*

Since 1601 Shakespeare had been writing less, and there were now a number of rival dramatists who were introducing new styles of drama, particularly Ben Jonson (whose first successful comedy, *Every Man in his Humour,* was acted by Shakespeare's company in 1598), Chapman, Dekker, Marston, and Beaumont and Fletcher who began to write in 1607. In 1608 the King's Men acquired a second playhouse, an indoor private theatre in the fashionable quarter of the Blackfriars. At private theatres, plays were performed indoors; the prices charged were higher than in the public playhouses, and the audience consequently was more select. Shakespeare seems to have retired from the stage about this time: his name does not occur in the various lists of players after 1607. Henceforward he lived for the most part at Stratford, where he was regarded as one of the most important citizens. He still wrote a few plays, and he tried his hand at the new form of tragi-comedy – a play with tragic incidents but a happy ending – which Beaumont and Fletcher had popularized. He wrote four of these – *Pericles, Cymbeline, The Winter's Tale,* and *The Tempest,* which was acted at Court in 1611. For the last four years of his life he lived in retirement. His son Hamnet had died in 1596: his two daughters were now married. Shakespeare died at Stratford upon Avon on April 23, 1616, and was buried in the chancel of the church, before the high altar. Shortly afterwards a memorial which still exists, with a portrait bust, was set up on the North wall. His wife survived him.

When Shakespeare died fourteen of his plays had been separately published in Quarto booklets. In 1623 his surviving fellow actors, John Heming and Henry Condell, with the co-operation of a number of printers, published a collected edition of thirty-six plays in one Folio volume, with an engraved portrait, memorial verses by Ben Jonson and others, and an Epistle to the Reader in which Heming and Condell make the interesting note that Shakespeare's 'hand and mind went together, and what he thought, he uttered with that easiness that we have scarce received from him a blot in his papers.'

The plays as printed in the Quartos or the Folio differ considerably from the usual modern text. They are often not divided into scenes, and sometimes not even into acts. Nor are there place-headings at the beginning of each scene, because in the Elizabethan theatre there was no scenery. They are carelessly printed and the spelling is erratic.

THE ELIZABETHAN THEATRE

Although plays of one sort and another had been acted for many generations, no permanent playhouse was erected in England until 1576. In the 1570s the Lord Mayor and Aldermen of the City of London and the players were constantly at variance. As a result James Burbage, then the leader of the great Earl of Leicester's players, decided that he would erect a playhouse outside the jurisdiction of the Lord Mayor, where the players would no longer be hindered by the authorities. Accordingly in 1576 he built the Theatre in Shoreditch, at that time a suburb of London. The experiment was successful, and by 1592 there were two more playhouses in London, the Curtain (also in Shoreditch), and the Rose on the south bank of the river, near Southwark Cathedral.

Elizabethan players were accustomed to act on a variety of stages; in the great hall of a nobleman's house, or one of the Queen's palaces, in town halls and in inn yards, as well as their own theatre.

The public playhouse for which most of Shakespeare's plays were written was a small and intimate affair. The outside measurement of the Fortune Theatre, which was built in 1600 to rival the new Globe, was but eighty feet square. Playhouses were usually circular or octagonal, with three tiers of galleries looking down upon the yard or pit, which was open to the sky. The stage jutted out into the yard so that the actors came forward into the midst of their audience.

Over the stage there was a roof, and on either side doors by which the characters entered or disappeared. Over the back of the stage ran a gallery or upper stage with windows on either side which was used when ever an upper scene was needed, as when Romeo climbs up to Juliet's bedroom, or the citizens of Angiers address King John from the walls. The space beneath this upper stage was known as the tiring house; it was concealed from the audience by a curtain which would be drawn back to reveal an inner stage, for such scenes as the witches' cave in *Macbeth*, Prospero's cell, or Juliet's tomb.

There was no general curtain concealing the whole stage, so that all scenes on the main stage began with an entrance and ended with an exit. Thus in tragedies the dead must be carried away. There was no scenery, and therefore no limit to the number of scenes, for a scene came to an end when the characters left the stage. When it was necessary for the exact locality of a scene to be known, then Shakespeare

THE GLOBE THEATRE

Wood-engraving by R. J. Beedham after a reconstruction by J. C. Adams

indicated it in the dialogue; otherwise a simple property or a garment was sufficient. A chair or stool showed an indoor scene, a man wearing riding boots was a messenger, a king wearing armour was on the battlefield, or the like. Such simplicity was on the whole an advantage; the spectator was not distracted by the setting and Shakespeare was able to use as many scenes as he wished. The action passed by very quickly: a play of 2500 lines of verse could be acted in two hours. Moreover since the actor was so close to his audience, the slightest subtlety of voice and gesture was easily appreciated.

The company was a 'Fellowship of Players', who were all partners and sharers. There were usually ten to fifteen full members, with three or four boys, and some paid servants. Shakespeare had therefore to write for his team. The chief actor in the company was Richard Burbage, who first distinguished himself as Richard III; for him Shakespeare wrote his great tragic parts. An important member of the company was the clown or low comedian. From 1594 to 1600 the company's clown was Will Kemp; he was succeeded by Robert Armin. No women were allowed to appear on the stage, and all women's parts were taken by boys.

THE FIRST PART OF THE
HISTORY OF HENRY THE FOURTH

The First Part of Henry the Fourth was probably written in the autumn of 1597. It was entered in the Stationers' Register on 25th February 1598 to Andrew Wise. The First Quarto of the play is entitled: *The History of Henrie the Fourth; With the battell at Shrewsburie, betweene the King and Lord Henry Percy, surnamed Henrie Hotspur of the North. With the humorous conceits of Sir John Falstaffe. At London, Printed by P.S. for Andrew Wise, dwelling in Paules Church-yard, at the signe of the Angell. 1598.* From the first it was the most popular of all Shakespeare's plays: six editions are known before the Folio of 1623 was published, dated 1598, 1599, 1604, 1608, 1613, 1622.

Henry the Fourth is the sequel to *Richard the Second*, and continues the story to show how Henry of Bolingbroke, by usurping the throne of his cousin Richard, brought sorrow and trouble on himself. *Richard the Second* was written about 1595: it was first published, also by Andrew Wise, in the early autumn of 1597, and went into three editions in a few months. The popularity of *Richard the Second* was not entirely due to literary excellence, though its poetry was much admired, but to certain meanings which were read into the story. In the late 1590s Shakespeare's contemporaries, for various reasons, thought that the story of Richard the Second and his deposition by Henry of Bolingbroke reflected on their own times: and the discontented followers of the Earl of Essex regarded him as a second Bolingbroke. The parallel was frequently made. Early in 1599 a young lawyer named John Hayward brought out a

History of The Life and Reign of Henry the Fourth, which related the events leading up to the deposition of Richard.
The book was considered so seditious in intention that
Hayward was imprisoned in the Tower. It is probable
therefore that Shakespeare was led to continue the story of
Henry of Bolingbroke by the success of Wise's publication
of *Richard the Second.*

As with *Richard the Second* and his other plays of English
history, Shakespeare took the outline and much of the de-
tail for the historical scenes from Ralph Holinshed's
Chronicles, which he adapted and expanded freely. For an
example, the beginning of the quarrel between King Henry
and the Percies (Act I Scenes 1 and 3) was related by
Holinshed thus:

'Henry, Earl of Northumberland, with his brother
Thomas, Earl of Worcester, and his son the Lord Henry
Percy surnamed Hotspur, which were to King Henry in
the beginning of his reign both faithful friends and earnest
aiders, began now to envy his wealth and felicity; and
especially they were grieved because the King demanded of the Earl and his son such Scottish prisoners as
were taken at Holmedon and Nesbit: for, of all the cap-
tives which were taken in the conflicts foughten in those
two places, there was delivered to the King's possession
only Mordake Earl of Fife, the Duke of Albany's son;
though the King did divers and sundry times require
deliverance of the residue, and that with great threaten-
ings: wherewith, the Percies being sore offended, (for
that they claimed them as their own proper prisoners,
and their peculiar prize,) by the counsel of the Lord
Thomas Percy, Earl of Worcester, whose study was ever
(as some write) to procure malice, and set things in a

broil, came to the King unto Windsor, (upon a purpose to prove him,) and there required of him, that either by ransom or otherwise, he would cause to be delivered out of prison Edmund Mortimer Earl of March, their cousin german, whom (as they reported) Owen Glendower kept in filthy prison, shackled with irons; only for that he took his part, and was to him faithful and true.

'The King began not a little to muse at this request, and not without cause: for indeed it touched him somewhat near, sith this Edmund was son to Roger Earl of March, son to the Lady Philip, daughter of Lionel, Duke of Clarence, the third son of King Edward the Third; which Edmund, at King Richard's going into Ireland, was proclaimed heir apparent to the Crown and realm; whose aunt, called Eleanor, the Lord Henry Percy had married; and therefore King Henry could not well bear that any man should be earnest about the advancement of that lineage. The King when he had studied on the matter, made answer, that the Earl of March was not taken prisoner for his cause, nor in his service, but willingly suffered himself to be taken, because he would not withstand the attempts of Owen Glendower and his complices; and therefore he would neither ransom him, nor relieve him.

'The Percies with this answer and fraudulent excuse were not a little fumed, insomuch that Henry Hotspur said openly: "Behold, the heir of the realm is robbed of his right, and yet the robber with his own will not redeem him!" So in this fury the Percies departed, minding nothing more than to depose King Henry from the high type of his royalty, and to place in his seat their cousin Edmund, Earl of March, whom they did not only deliver out of captivity, but also (to the high displeasure of King Henry) entered in league with the foresaid Owen Glendower.'

The comic scenes of Prince Henry and Falstaff were mostly Shakespeare's own invention. The Prince had the reputation of being a wild youth. According to Stow's Chronicle,

'he lived somewhat insolently, insomuch that, whilst his father lived, being accompanied with some of his young lords and gentlemen, he would wait in disguised array for his own receivers, and distress them of their money; and sometimes at such enterprises both he and his company were surely beaten; and when his receivers made to him their complaints how they were robbed in their coming to him, he would give them discharge of so much money as they had lost; and, besides that, they should not depart from him without great rewards for their trouble and vexation; especially they should be rewarded that best had resisted him, and his company, and of whom he had received the most and greatest strokes.'

[*Shakespeare's Holinshed*, by W. G. Boswell-Stone. VI.]

Prince Hal was also a popular character on the stage, and a robbing on Gadshill was one of the better scenes in an old play called *The Famous Victories of Henry the Fifth*, where the Prince's companion in mischief is called Sir John Oldcastle. Shakespeare at first took over the name, and called his fat knight 'Sir John Oldcastle.' This caused trouble. The original Sir John Oldcastle, who was styled Lord Cobham, had been burnt for his Lollard principles and seditious practices in the reign of Henry V, and had thus come to be regarded as an early Protestant martyr. The Lord Cobham of Shakespeare's day had newly succeeded to the title. He was much annoyed that his distinguished predecessor should appear upon a public stage in such a disreputable guise. The name was accordingly altered to Falstaff. There are still slight traces of this revision, especially in the second part of the play.

Falstaff was a caricature of a common Elizabethan type, the dishonest professional captain, who waxed fat during the continual wars of 1587–1603. In the autumn of 1597 when Shakespeare was writing the play London was full of these captains newly returned with the Earl of Essex from the expedition to the Azores.

> 'Captains about town spent generously whilst funds lasted upon taverns, harlots and players, and some of them ran to fat. Many were gentlemen of good, and even of noble, family and excellent education who preferred the excitement of the wars to a life compounded of farming, hunting, occasional lawsuits in London, and the local dignity of Justice of the peace. They were queer characters with flamboyant clothes, hasty tempers, blustering manners, and vocabularies of unfathomable richness; and at the return of the expedition many of them were let loose on the City.' [*Shakespeare at Work*, p. 130.]

The Quarto of the play which Andrew Wise published in 1598 is a good text, and the later quartos and the Folio derive from it. There are no divisions into Acts and Scenes. The punctuation is light but effective, and there are not many errors. In the present text the First Quarto has been followed closely, and its few errors have been corrected by the Folio text. Spelling is modernized, but the original arrangement, and the punctuation (which according to Elizabethan practice 'points' the text for reading aloud) have been kept, except where they seemed obviously wrong. The reader who is used to an 'accepted text' may thus find certain unfamiliarities, but the present text is nearer to that used in Shakespeare's own playhouse.

The First Part of the History of Henry the Fourth

THE ACTORS' NAMES

KING HENRY the Fourth.
HENRY, Prince of Wales } sons to the King.
JOHN of Lancaster
EARL OF WESTMORELAND.
SIR WALTER BLUNT.
THOMAS PERCY, Earl of Worcester.
HENRY PERCY, Earl of Northumberland.
HENRY PERCY, surnamed HOTSPUR, his son.
EDMUND MORTIMER, Earl of March.
RICHARD SCROOP, Archbishop of York.
ARCHIBALD, Earl of Douglas.
OWEN GLENDOWER.
SIR RICHARD VERNON.
SIR JOHN FALSTAFF.
SIR MICHAEL, a friend to the Archbishop of York.
POINS.
GADSHILL.
PETO.
BARDOLPH.
Two Carriers.
Travellers.
Sheriff.
Vintner.
Chamberlain.
Two Drawers.

LADY PERCY, wife to Hotspur, and sister to Mortimer.
LADY MORTIMER, daughter to Glendower, and wife to
    Mortimer.
MISTRESS QUICKLY, hostess of a tavern in Eastcheap.

Enter King Henry, Lord John of Lancaster, Earl of Westmore-
land, Sir Walter Blunt, with others.

KING: So shaken as we are, so wan with care,
 Find we a time for frighted peace to pant,
 And breathe short winded accents of new broils
 To be commenc'd in stronds afar remote:
 No more the thirsty entrance of this soil
 Shall daub her lips with her own children's blood,
 No more shall trenching war channel her fields,
 Nor bruise her flowrets with the armed hoofs
 Of hostile paces: those opposed eyes,
 Which like the meteors of a troubled heaven,
 All of one nature, of one substance bred,
 Did lately meet in the intestine shock
 And furious close of civil butchery,
 Shall now in mutual well-beseeming ranks,
 March all one way, and be no more oppos'd
 Against acquaintance, kindred and allies.
 The edge of war, like an ill-sheathed knife,
 No more shall cut his master: therefore friends,
 As far as to the sepulchre of Christ,
 Whose soldier now, under whose blessed cross
 We are impressed and engag'd to fight,
 Forthwith a power of English shall we levy,
 Whose arms were moulded in their mothers' womb,
 To chase these pagans in those holy fields,
 Over whose acres walk'd those blessed feet,
 Which fourteen hundred years ago were nail'd,
 For our advantage on the bitter cross.

But this our purpose now is twelve month old,
And bootless 'tis to tell you we will go.
Therefore we meet not now: then let me hear
Of you my gentle Cousin Westmoreland,
What yesternight our council did decree
In forwarding this dear expedience.

WESTMORELAND: My liege, this haste was hot in ques-
tion,
And many limits of the charge set down
But yesternight, when all athwart there came
A post from Wales, loaden with heavy news,
Whose worst was that the noble Mortimer,
Leading the men of Herefordshire to fight
Against the irregular, and wild Glendower,
Was by the rude hands of that Welchman taken,
A thousand of his people butchered,
Upon whose dead corpse there was such misuse,
Such beastly shameless transformation
By those Welch-women done, as may not be
Without much shame, retold, or spoken of.

KING: It seems then that the tidings of this broil,
Brake off our business for the Holy Land.

WESTMORELAND: This match'd with other did, my gra-
cious Lord.
For more uneven and unwelcome news
Came from the North, and thus it did import,
On Holy-rood day the gallant Hotspur there,
Young Harry Percy, and brave Archibald,
That ever valiant and approved Scot,
At Holmedon met, where they did spend
A sad and bloody hour:
As by discharge of their artillery,
And shape of likelihood the news was told:

For he that brought them in the very heat
And pride of their contention, did take horse
Uncertain of the issue any way.

KING: Here is a dear, true industrious friend,
Sir Walter Blunt new lighted from his horse,
Stain'd with the variation of each soil,
Betwixt that Holmedon and this seat of ours:
And he hath brought us smooth and welcome news,
The Earl of Douglas is discomfited,
Ten thousand bold Scots, two and twenty knights
Balk'd in their own blood did Sir Walter see
On Holmedon's plains: of prisoners Hotspur took
Mordake Earl of Fife, and eldest son
To beaten Douglas, and the Earl of Athol,
Of Murray, Angus, and Menteith:
And is not this an honourable spoil?
A gallant prize? Ha cousin, is it not? In faith it is.

WESTMORELAND: A conquest for a Prince to boast of.

KING: Yea, there thou mak'st me sad, and mak'st me sin
In envy, that my Lord Northumberland
Should be the father to so blest a son:
A son, who is the theme of honour's tongue,
Amongst a grove, the very straightest plant,
Who is sweet fortune's minion and her pride,
Whilst I by looking on the praise of him
See riot and dishonour stain the brow
Of my young Harry. O that it could be prov'd
That some night tripping fairy had exchang'd
In cradle clothes our children where they lay,
And call'd mine Percy, his Plantagenet,
Then would I have his Harry, and he mine:
But let him from my thoughts. What think you coz
Of this young Percy's pride? The prisoners

Which he in this adventure hath surpris'd
To his own use, he keeps and sends me word
I shall have none but Mordake Earl of Fife.

WESTMORELAND: This is his uncle's teaching. This is
  Worcester,
  Malevolent to you in all aspects,
  Which makes him prune himself, and bristle up
  The crest of youth against your dignity.

KING: But I have sent for him to answer this:
  And for this cause awhile we must neglect
  Our holy purpose to Jerusalem.
  Cousin on Wednesday next our council we
  Will hold at Windsor, so inform the Lords:
  But come yourself with speed to us again,
  For more is to be said and to be done,
  Than out of anger can be uttered.

WESTMORELAND: I will my liege.

Exeunt.

I.2

Enter Prince of Wales, and Sir John Falstaff.

FALSTAFF: Now Hal, what time of day is it lad?

PRINCE: Thou art so fat-witted with drinking of old
  sack, and unbuttoning thee after supper, and sleeping
  upon benches after noon; that thou has forgotten to
  demand that truly which thou wouldest truly know.
  What a devil hast thou to do with the time of the day?
  unless hours were cups of sack, and minutes capons, and
  clocks the tongues of bawds, and dials the signs of leap-
  ing houses, and the blessed sun himself a fair hot wench
  in flame-coloured taffeta; I see no reason why thou

shouldst be so superfluous to demand the time of the day.

FALSTAFF: Indeed you come near me now Hal, for we that take purses go by the moon and the seven stars, and not by Phoebus, he, that wand'ring knight so fair: and I prithee sweet wag when thou art a king as God save thy grace: majesty I should say, for grace thou wilt have none.

PRINCE: What none?

FALSTAFF: No by my troth, not so much as will serve to be prologue to an egg and butter.

PRINCE: Well, how then? come roundly, roundly.

FALSTAFF: Marry then sweet wag, when thou art king let not us that are squires of the night's body, be called thieves of the day's beauty: let us be Diana's foresters, gentlemen of the shade, minions of the moon, and let men say we be men of good government, being governed as the sea is, by our noble and chaste mistress the moon, under whose countenance we steal.

PRINCE: Thou sayest well, and it holds well too, for the fortune of us that are the moon's men, doth ebb and flow like the sea, being governed as the sea is by the moon. As for proof, now a purse of gold most resolutely snatch'd on Monday night and most dissolutely spent on Tuesday morning, got with swearing, lay by, and spent with crying, bring in, now in as low an ebb as the foot of the ladder, and by and by in as high a flow as the ridge of the gallows.

FALSTAFF: By the Lord thou sayest true lad, and is not my hostess of the tavern a most sweet wench?

PRINCE: As the honey of Hybla my old lad of the castle, and is not a buff jerkin a most sweet robe of durance?

FALSTAFF: How now, how now mad wag, what in thy

quips and thy quiddities? what a plague have I to do with a buff jerkin?

PRINCE: Why what a pox have I to do with my hostess of the tavern?

FALSTAFF: Well, thou hast call'd her to a reckoning many a time and oft.

PRINCE: Did I ever call for thee to pay thy part?

FALSTAFF: No, I'll give thee thy due, thou has paid all there.

PRINCE: Yea and elsewhere, so far as my coin would stretch, and where it would not, I have used my credit.

FALSTAFF: Yea, and so us'd it that were it not here apparent that thou art heir apparent. But I prithee sweet wag, shall there be gallows standing in England when thou art king? and resolution thus fubb'd as it is with the rusty curb of old father Antic the law, do not thou when thou art king hang a thief.

PRINCE: No, thou shalt.

FALSTAFF: Shall I? O rare! by the Lord I'll be a brave judge.

PRINCE: Thou judgest false already, I mean thou shalt have the hanging of the thieves, and so become a rare hangman.

FALSTAFF: Well Hal well, and in some sort it jumps with my humour, as well as waiting in the Court I can tell you.

PRINCE: For obtaining of suits?

FALSTAFF: Yea, for obtaining of suits, whereof the hangman hath no lean wardrobe. 'Sblood I am as melancholy as a gib cat, or a lugg'd bear.

PRINCE: Or an old lion, or a lover's lute.

FALSTAFF: Yea, or the drone of a Lincolnshire bagpipe.

PRINCE: What sayest thou to a hare, or the melancholy of Moorditch?

FALSTAFF: Thou hast the most unsavoury similes, and art

indeed the most comparative rascalliest sweet young Prince. But Hal, I prithee trouble me no more with vanity, I would to God thou and I knew where a commodity of good names were to be bought: an old Lord of the Council rated me the other day in the street about you sir, but I mark'd him not, and yet he talk'd very wisely, but I regarded him not, and yet he talk'd wisely and in the street too.

PRINCE: Thou didst well, for wisdom cries out in the streets and no man regards it.

FALSTAFF: O thou hast damnable iteration, and art indeed able to corrupt a saint: thou hast done much harm upon me Hal, God forgive thee for it: before I knew thee Hal I knew nothing, and now am I, if a man should speak truly, little better than one of the wicked: I must give over this life, and I will give it over: by the Lord and I do not, I am a villain, I'll be damn'd for never a king's son in Christendom.

PRINCE: Where shall we take a purse tomorrow Jack?

FALSTAFF: 'Zounds where thou wilt lad, I'll make one, an I do not call me villain and baffle me.

PRINCE: I see a good amendment of life in thee, from praying to purse-taking.

FALSTAFF: Why Hal, 'tis my vocation Hal, 'tis no sin for a man to labour in his vocation.

Enter Poins.

Poins: now shall we know if Gadshill have set a match. O if men were to be saved by merit, what hole in hell were hot enough for him? this is the most omnipotent villain that ever cried, stand, to a true man.

PRINCE: Good morrow Ned.

POINS: Good morrow sweet Hal. What says Monsieur Remorse? what says Sir John Sack, and Sugar, Jack?

how agrees the Devil and thee about thy soul that thou soldest him on Good Friday last, for a cup of Madeira and a cold capon's leg?

PRINCE: Sir John stands to his word, the devil shall have his bargain, for he was never yet a breaker of proverbs: he will give the devil his due.

POINS: Then art thou damn'd for keeping thy word with the devil.

PRINCE: Else he had been damn'd for cozening the devil.

POINS: But my lads, my lads, tomorrow morning, by four o'clock early at Gadshill, there are pilgrims going to Canterbury with rich offerings, and traders riding to London with fat purses. I have vizards for you all, you have horses for yourselves, Gadshill lies tonight in Rochester, I have bespoke supper tomorrow night in Eastcheap: we may do it as secure as sleep, if you will go I will stuff your purses full of crowns: if you will not, tarry at home and be hang'd.

FALSTAFF: Hear ye Yedward, if I tarry at home and go not, I'll hang you for going.

POINS: You will chops.

FALSTAFF: Hal wilt thou make one?

PRINCE: Who I rob, I a thief? not I by my faith.

FALSTAFF: There's neither honesty, manhood, nor good fellowship in thee, nor thou cam'st not of the blood royal, if thou darest not stand for ten shillings.

PRINCE: Well then, once in my days I'll be a madcap.

FALSTAFF: Why that's well said.

PRINCE: Well, come what will, I'll tarry at home.

FALSTAFF: By the Lord, I'll be a traitor then, when thou art king.

PRINCE: I care not.

POINS: Sir John, I prithee leave the prince and me alone,

I will lay him down such reasons for this adventure that he shall go.

FALSTAFF: Well God give thee the spirit of persuasion, and him the ears of profiting, that what thou speakest, may move, and what he hears, may be believed, that the true prince may (for recreation sake,) prove a false thief, for the poor abuses of the time want countenance: farewell, you shall find me in Eastcheap.

PRINCE: Farewell the latter spring, farewell All-hallown summer.

Exit Falstaff.

POINS: Now my good sweet honey Lord, ride with us tomorrow. I have a jest to execute, that I cannot manage alone. Falstaff, Bardolph, Peto, and Gadshill, shall rob those men that we have already waylaid, yourself and I will not be there: and when they have the booty, if you and I do not rob them, cut this head off from my shoulders.

PRINCE: How shall we part with them in setting forth?

POINS: Why, we will set forth before or after them, and appoint them a place of meeting, wherein it is at our pleasure to fail; and then will they adventure upon the exploit themselves, which they shall have no sooner achieved but we 'll set upon them.

PRINCE: Yea but 'tis like that they will know us by our horses, by our habits, and by every other appointment to be ourselves.

POINS: Tut, our horses they shall not see, I 'll tie them in the wood, our vizards we will change after we leave them: and sirrah, I have cases of buckram for the nonce, to inmask our noted outward garments.

PRINCE: Yea, but I doubt they will be too hard for us.

POINS: Well, for two of them, I know them to be as

true bred cowards as ever turn'd back: and for the
third, if he fight longer than he sees reason, I 'll forswear
arms. The virtue of this jest will be the incomprehensible
lies, that this same fat rogue will tell us when we meet at
supper, how thirty at least he fought with, what wards,
what blows, what extremities he endured, and in the reproof of this lives the jest.

PRINCE: Well, I 'll go with thee, provide us all things
necessary, and meet me tomorrow night in Eastcheap,
there I 'll sup: farewell.

POINS: Farewell my Lord.

Exit Poins.

PRINCE: I know you all, and will a while uphold
The unyok'd humour of your idleness,
Yet herein will I imitate the sun,
Who doth permit the base contagious clouds
To smother up his beauty from the world,
That when he please again to be himself,
Being wanted he may be more wonder'd at
By breaking through the foul and ugly mists
Of vapours that did seem to strangle him.
If all the year were playing holy-days,
To sport would be as tedious as to work;
But when they seldom come, they wish'd for come,
And nothing pleaseth but rare accidents:
So when this loose behaviour I throw off,
And pay the debt I never promised,
By how much better than my word I am,
By so much shall I falsify men's hopes,
And like bright metal on a sullen ground,
My reformation glittering o'er my fault,
Shall show more goodly, and attract more eyes
Than that which hath no foil to set it off.

I 'll so offend, to make offence a skill,
Redeeming time when men think least I will.
                              Exit.

I. 3

*Enter the King, Northumberland, Worcester, Hotspur,
Sir Walter Blunt, with others.*

KING: My blood hath been too cold and temperate,
  Unapt to stir at these indignities,
  And you have found me, for accordingly
  You tread upon my patience, but be sure
  I will from henceforth rather be myself
  Mighty, and to be fear'd, than my condition
  Which hath been smooth as oil, soft as young down,
  And therefore lost that title of respect,
  Which the proud soul ne'er pays but to the proud.
WORCESTER: Our house (my sovereign liege) little deserves
  The scourge of greatness to be us'd on it,
  And that same greatness too, which our own hands
  Have holp to make so portly.
NORTHUMBERLAND: My Lord.
KING: Worcester get thee gone, for I do see
  Danger, and disobedience in thine eye:
  O sir, your presence is too bold and peremptory,
  And Majesty might never yet endure
  The moody frontier of a servant brow,
  You have good leave to leave us, when we need
  Your use and counsel we shall send for you.
                              Exit Worcester.
  You were about to speak.
NORTHUMBERLAND: Yea my good Lord.
  Those prisoners in your Highness' name demanded,

B

Which Harry Percy here at Holmedon took,
Were as he says, not with such strength denied
As is delivered to your Majesty.
Either envy therefore, or misprision,
Is guilty of this fault, and not my son.
HOTSPUR: My liege, I did deny no prisoners,
But I remember when the fight was done,
When I was dry with rage, and extreme toil,
Breathless and faint, leaning upon my sword,
Came there a certain Lord, neat and trimly dress'd,
Fresh as a bridegroom, and his chin new reap'd,
Show'd like a stubble-land at harvest home,
He was perfumed like a milliner,
And 'twixt his finger and his thumb he held
A pouncet box, which ever and anon
He gave his nose, and took 't away again,
Who therewith angry, when it next came there
Took it in snuff, and still he smil'd and talk'd:
And as the soldiers bore dead bodies by,
He call'd them untaught knaves, unmannerly,
To bring a slovenly unhandsome corse
Betwixt the wind and his nobility:
With many holy-day and lady terms
He questioned me, amongst the rest demanded
My prisoners in your Majesty's behalf.
I then, all smarting with my wounds being cold,
To be so pester'd with a popinjay,
Out of my grief and my impatience
Answer'd neglectingly, I know not what
He should, or he should not, for he made me mad
To see him shine so brisk, and smell so sweet,
And talk so like a waiting gentlewoman,
Of guns, and drums, and wounds, God save the mark:

And telling me the sovereignest thing on earth
Was parmaceti, for an inward bruise,
And that it was great pity, so it was,
This villainous saltpetre, should be digg'd
Out of the bowels of the harmless earth,
Which many a good tall fellow had destroyed
So cowardly, and but for these vile guns
He would himself have been a soldier.
This bald unjointed chat of his (my Lord)
I answered indirectly (as I said)
And I beseech you, let not his report
Come current for an accusation
Betwixt my love and your high majesty.
BLUNT: The circumstance considered, good my lord,
Whate'er Lord Harry Percy then had said
To such a person, and in such a place,
At such a time, with all the rest re-told,
May reasonably die, and never rise
To do him wrong, or any way impeach
What then he said, so he unsay it now.
KING: Why yet he doth deny his prisoners,
But with proviso and exception,
That we at our own charge shall ransom straight
His brother-in-law, the foolish Mortimer,
Who on my soul, hath wilfully betray'd
The lives of those, that he did lead to fight
Against that great Magician, damn'd Glendower,
Whose daughter as we hear, that Earl of March
Hath lately married: shall our coffers then
Be emptied, to redeem a traitor home?
Shall we buy treason? and indent with fears
When they have lost and forfeited themselves:
No, on the barren mountains let him starve:

For I shall never hold that man my friend,
Whose tongue shall ask me for one penny cost
To ransom home revolted Mortimer.
HOTSPUR: Revolted Mortimer:
He never did fall off, my sovereign liege
But by the chance of war, to prove that true
Needs no more but one tongue: for all those wounds,
Those mouthed wounds which valiantly he took,
When on the gentle Severn's sedgy bank,
In single opposition hand to hand,
He did confound the best part of an hour,
In changing hardiment with great Glendower:
Three times they breath'd and three times did they drink
Upon agreement of swift Severn's flood,
Who then affrighted with their bloody looks,
Ran fearfully among the trembling reeds,
And hid his crisp head in the hollow bank,
Bloodstained with these valiant combatants,
Never did base and rotten policy
Colour her working with such deadly wounds,
Nor never could the noble Mortimer
Receive so many, and all willingly,
Then let not him be slandered with revolt.
KING: Thou dost belie him Percy, thou dost belie him,
He never did encounter with Glendower:
I tell thee, he durst as well have met the devil alone,
As Owen Glendower for an enemy.
Art thou not asham'd? but sirrah, henceforth
Let me not hear you speak of Mortimer:
Send me your prisoners with the speediest means,
Or you shall hear in such a kind from me
As will displease you. My Lord Northumberland:
We license your departure with your son,

Send us your prisoners, or you will hear of it.
Exeunt King, and train.
HOTSPUR: And if the devil come and roar for them
I will not send them: I will after straight
And tell him so, for I will ease my heart,
Albeit I make a hazard of my head.
NORTHUMBERLAND: What? drunk with choler, stay, and pause a while,
Here comes your uncle.
Enter Worcester.
HOTSPUR: Speak of Mortimer?
'Zounds I will speak of him, and let my soul
Want mercy if I do not join with him:
Yea on his part, I 'll empty all these veins,
And shed my dear blood, drop by drop in the dust,
But I will lift the down-trod Mortimer
As high in the air as this unthankful king,
As this ingrate and canker'd Bolingbroke.
NORTHUMBERLAND: Brother, the king hath made your nephew mad.
WORCESTER: Who struck this heat up after I was gone?
HOTSPUR: He will forsooth have all my prisoners,
And when I urg'd the ransom once again
Of my wife's brother, then his cheek look'd pale,
And on my face he turn'd an eye of death,
Trembling even at the name of Mortimer.
WORCESTER: I cannot blame him, was not he proclaim'd
By Richard that dead is, the next of blood?
NORTHUMBERLAND: He was, I heard the proclamation:
And then it was, when the unhappy king,
(Whose wrongs in us God pardon) did set forth
Upon his Irish expedition:
From whence he intercepted, did return

To be depos'd, and shortly murdered.

WORCESTER: And for whose death, we in the world's
wide mouth
Live scandaliz'd and foully spoken of.

HOTSPUR: But soft, I pray you did King Richard then
Proclaim my brother Edmund Mortimer
Heir to the crown?

NORTHUMBERLAND: He did, myself did hear it.

HOTSPUR: Nay then I cannot blame his cousin king,
That wish'd him on the barren mountains starve.
But shall it be that you that set the crown
Upon the head of this forgetful man,
And for his sake wear the detested blot
Of murtherous subornation? shall it be
That you a world of curses undergo,
Being the agents, or base second means,
The cords, the ladder, or the hangman rather,
O pardon me, that I descend so low,
To show the line and the predicament,
Wherein you range under this subtle king!
Shall it for shame be spoken in these days,
Or fill up Chronicles in time to come,
That men of your nobility and power
Did gage them both in an unjust behalf,
(As both of you, God pardon it, have done)
To put down Richard, that sweet lovely rose,
And plant this thorn, this canker Bolingbroke?
And shall it in more shame be further spoken,
That you are fool'd, discarded, and shook off
By him, for whom these shames ye underwent?
No, yet time serves, wherein you may redeem
Your banish'd honours, and restore yourselves
Into the good thoughts of the world again:

Revenge the jeering and disdain'd contempt
Of this proud king, who studies day and night
To answer all the debt he owes to you,
Even with the bloody payment of your deaths:
Therefore I say.

WORCESTER: Peace cousin, say no more.
And now I will unclasp a secret book,
And to your quick conceiving discontents
I 'll read you matter deep and dangerous,
As full of peril and adventurous spirit,
As to o'erwalk a current roaring loud,
On the unsteadfast footing of a spear.

HOTSPUR: If he fall in, good night, or sink, or swim,
Send danger from the East unto the West,
So honour cross it, from the North to South,
And let them grapple: O the blood more stirs
To rouse a lion than to start a hare.

NORTHUMBERLAND: Imagination of some great exploit
Drives him beyond the bounds of patience.

HOTSPUR: By heaven methinks it were an easy leap,
To pluck bright honour from the pale-fac'd moon,
Or dive into the bottom of the deep,
Where fadomline could never touch the ground,
And pluck up drowned honour by the locks,
So he that doth redeem her thence might wear
Without corrival all her dignities,
But out upon this half-fac'd fellowship.

WORCESTER: He apprehends a world of figures here,
But not the form of what he should attend,
Good cousin give me audience for a while.

HOTSPUR: I cry you mercy.

WORCESTER: Those same noble Scots that are your
prisoners.

HOTSPUR: I 'll keep them all;
  By God he shall not have a Scot of them,
  No, if a Scot would save his soul he shall not.
  I 'll keep them by this hand.
WORCESTER: You start away,
  And lend no ear unto my purposes:
  Those prisoners you shall keep.
HOTSPUR: Nay I will: that 's flat:
  He said he would not ransom Mortimer,
  Forbad my tongue to speak of Mortimer,
  But I will find him when he lies asleep,
  And in his ear I 'll holla Mortimer:
  Nay, I 'll have a starling shall be taught to speak
  Nothing but Mortimer, and give it him
  To keep his anger still in motion.
WORCESTER: Hear you cousin a word.
HOTSPUR: All studies here I solemnly defy,
  Save how to gall and pinch this Bolingbroke,
  And that same sword and buckler Prince of Wales,
  But that I think his father loves him not,
  And would be glad he met with some mischance:
  I would have him poisoned with a pot of ale.
WORCESTER: Farewell kinsman, I 'll talk to you
  When you are better temper'd to attend.
NORTHUMBERLAND: Why what a wasp-stung and im-
    patient fool
  Art thou? to break into this woman's mood,
  Tying thine ear to no tongue but thine own?
HOTSPUR: Why look you, I am whipp'd and scourg'd
    with rods,
  Nettled, and stung with pismires, when I hear
  Of this vile politician Bolingbroke,
  In Richard's time, what do you call the place?

A plague upon it, it is in Gloucestershire;
'Twas where the madcap duke his uncle kept,
His Uncle York, where I first bowed my knee
Unto this king of smiles, this Bolingbroke:
'Zblood, when you and he came back from Ravens-
purgh.

NORTHUMBERLAND: At Berkley-castle.

HOTSPUR: You say true.
Why what a candy deal of courtesy,
This fawning greyhound then did proffer me,
Look when his infant fortune came to age,
And gentle Harry Percy, and kind cousin:
O the devil take such cozeners, God forgive me,
Good uncle tell your tale, I have done.

WORCESTER: Nay, if you have not, to it again,
We will stay your leisure.

HOTSPUR: I have done i' faith.

WORCESTER: Then once more to your Scottish prisoners,
Deliver them up without their ransom straight,
And make the Douglas' son your only mean
For powers in Scotland, which for divers reasons
Which I shall send you written, be assur'd
Will easily be granted you my Lord,
Your son in Scotland being thus employed,
Shall secretly into the bosom creep
Of that same noble prelate well-belov'd,
The Archbishop.

HOTSPUR: Of York, is it not?

WORCESTER: True, who bears hard
His brother's death at Bristow, the Lord Scroop,
I speak not this in estimation,
As what I think might be, but what I know
Is ruminated, plotted, and set down,

And only stays but to behold the face
Of that occasion that shall bring it on.

HOTSPUR: I smell it. Upon my life it will do well.

NORTHUMBERLAND: Before the game is afoot thou still
let'st slip.

HOTSPUR: Why, it cannot choose but be a noble plot,
And then the power of Scotland, and of York,
To join with Mortimer, ha.

WORCESTER: And so they shall.

HOTSPUR: In faith it is exceedingly well aim'd.

WORCESTER: And 'tis no little reason bids us speed,
To save our heads by raising of a head,
For bear ourselves as even as we can,
The king will always think him in our debt,
And think we think ourselves unsatisfied,
Till he hath found a time to pay us home.
And see already how he doth begin
To make us strangers to his looks of love.

HOTSPUR: He does, he does, we 'll be reveng'd on him.

WORCESTER: Cousin farewell. No further go in this,
Than I by letters shall direct your course.
When time is ripe, which will be suddenly,
I 'll steal to Glendower, and Lord Mortimer,
Where you and Douglas, and our powers at once,
As I will fashion it shall happily meet,
To bear our fortunes in our own strong arms,
Which now we hold at much uncertainty.

NORTHUMBERLAND: Farewell good brother, we shall
thrive I trust.

HOTSPUR: Uncle adieu: O let the hours be short,
Till fields, and blows, and groans, applaud our sport.

Exeunt.

Enter a Carrier with a lantern in his hand.

1 CARRIER: Heigh ho. An it be not four by the day I 'll
be hang'd, Charles' wain is over the new chimney, and
yet our horse not pack'd. What Ostler.

OSTLER: Anon, anon.

1 CARRIER: I prithee Tom beat Cut's saddle, put a few
flocks in the point, poor jade is wrung in the withers,
out of all cess.

Enter another Carrier.

2 CARRIER: Peas and beans are as dank here as a dog and
that is the next way to give poor jades the bots: this
house is turned upside down since Robin Ostler died.

1 CARRIER: Poor fellow never joyed since the price of
oats rose, it was the death of him.

2 CARRIER: I think this be the most villainous house in all
London road for fleas, I am stung like a tench.

1 CARRIER: Like a tench, by the Mass there is ne'er a
King christen could be better bit than I have been since
the first cock.

2 CARRIER: Why they will allow us ne'er a jordan, and
then we leak in your chimney, and your chamber-lie
breeds fleas like a loach.

1 CARRIER: What Ostler, come away and be hang'd,
come away.

2 CARRIER: I have a gammon of bacon, and two razes of
ginger, to be delivered as far as Charingcross.

1 CARRIER: God's body, the turkeys in my pannier are
quite starved: what ostler? a plague on thee, hast thou
never an eye in thy head? canst not hear, and 'twere not

as good deed as drink to break the pate on thee, I am a
very villain, come and be hang'd, hast no faith in thee?

Enter Gadshill.

GADSHILL: Good morrow Carriers, what 's a clock?

1 CARRIER: I think it be two a clock.

GADSHILL: I prithee lend me thy lantern, to see my
gelding in the stable.

1 CARRIER: Nay by God soft, I know a trick worth two
of that i' faith.

GADSHILL: I pray thee lend me thine.

2 CARRIER: Ay when canst tell? lend me thy lantern
(quoth he) marry I 'll see thee hang'd first.

GADSHILL: Sirrah Carrier, what time do you mean to
come to London?

2 CARRIER: Time enough to go to bed with a candle,
I warrant thee, come neighbour Mugs, we 'll call up
the gentlemen, they will along with company, for they
have great charge.

Exeunt Carriers.

Enter Chamberlain.

GADSHILL: What ho: Chamberlain.

CHAMBERLAIN: At hand quoth pickpurse.

GADSHILL: That 's even as fair as at hand quoth the
Chamberlain: for thou variest no more from picking
of purses, than giving direction doth from labouring:
thou layest the plot, how.

CHAMBERLAIN: Good morrow Master Gadshill, it holds
current that I told you yesternight, there 's a Franklin in
the wild of Kent hath brought three hundred marks with
him in gold, I heard him tell it to one of his company last
night at supper, a kind of Auditor, one that hath abund-
ance of charge too, God knows what, they are up already,
and call for eggs and butter, they will away presently.

GADSHILL: Sirrah, if they meet not with Saint Nicholas'
clerks, I 'll give thee this neck.

CHAMBERLAIN: No, I 'll none of it, I pray thee keep that
for the hangman, for I know thou worshippest Saint
Nicholas, as truly as a man of falsehood may.

GADSHILL: What talkest thou to me of the hangman?
if I hang, I 'll make a fat pair of gallows: for if I hang,
old Sir John hangs with me, and thou knowest he is no
starveling: tut, there are other Trojans that thou
dream'st not of, the which for sport sake are content to
do the profession some grace, that would (if matters
should be look'd into) for their own credit sake make all
whole. I am joined with no foot land-rakers, no long-staff
sixpenny strikers, none of these mad mustachio purple-
hued maltworms, but with nobility, and tranquillity,
Burgomasters and great Oneyers, such as can hold in, such
as will strike sooner than speak, and speak sooner than
drink, and drink sooner than pray, and yet ('zounds) I
lie, for they pray continually to their Saint the Common-
wealth, or rather not pray to her, but prey on her, for they
ride up and down on her, and make her their boots.

CHAMBERLAIN: What, the Common-wealth their boots?
will she hold out water in foul way?

GADSHILL: She will, she will, Justice hath liquor'd her:
we steal as in a castle cocksure: we have the receipt
of fernseed, we walk invisible.

CHAMBERLAIN: Nay by my faith, I think you are more
beholding to the night than to fernseed, for your
walking invisible.

GADSHILL: Give me thy hand, thou shalt have a share in
our purchase, as I am a true man.

CHAMBERLAIN: Nay rather let me have it, as you are a
false thief.

GADSHILL: Go to, *homo* is a common name to all men: bid the Ostler bring my gelding out of the stable, farewell you muddy knave.

Exeunt.

II. 2

Enter Prince and Poins.

POINS: Come shelter, shelter, I have remov'd Falstaff's horse, and he frets like a gumm'd velvet.

PRINCE: Stand close.

Enter Falstaff.

FALSTAFF: Poins, Poins, and be hang'd Poins.

PRINCE: Peace ye fat-kidney'd rascal, what a brawling dost thou keep?

FALSTAFF: Where 's Poins Hal?

PRINCE: He is walk'd up to the top of the hill, I 'll go seek him.

FALSTAFF: I am accurs'd to rob in that thief's company. The rascal hath removed my horse, and tied him I know not where, if I travel but four foot by the squire further afoot, I shall break my wind. Well, I doubt not but to die a fair death for all this, if I 'scape hanging for killing that rogue. I have forsworn his company hourly any time this two and twenty years, and yet I am bewitch'd with the rogue's company. If the rascal have not given me medicines to make me love him, I 'll be hang'd. It could not be else, I have drunk medicines, Poins, Hal, a plague upon you both. Bardolph, Peto, I 'll starve ere I 'll rob a foot further, and 'twere not as good a deed as drink to turn true man, and to leave these rogues, I am the veriest varlet that ever chewed with a tooth: eight yards of uneven ground is threescore and ten miles afoot with me, and the stony hearted villains know it well enough, a plague upon it when thieves cannot be true one to another:

They whistle.

Whew, a plague upon you all, give me my horse you rogues, give me my horse and be hang'd.

PRINCE: Peace ye fat guts, lie down, lay thine ear close to the ground, and list if thou canst hear the tread of travellers.

FALSTAFF: Have you any levers to lift me up again being down, 'zblood I 'll not bear mine own flesh so far afoot again for all the coin in thy father's Exchequer: What a plague mean ye to colt me thus?

PRINCE: Thou liest, thou art not colted, thou art uncolted.

FALSTAFF: I prithee good prince, Hal, help me to my horse, good king's son.

PRINCE: Out ye rogue shall I be your Ostler?

FALSTAFF: Hang thyself in thine own heir apparent garters, if I be ta'en, I 'll peach for this: and I have not ballads made on you all, and sung to filthy tunes, let a cup of sack be my poison, when a jest is so forward, and afoot too I hate it.

Enter Gadshill, Bardolph and Peto with him.

GADSHILL: Stand.

FALSTAFF: So I do against my will.

POINS: O 'tis our setter, I know his voice, Bardolph, what news.

BARDOLPH: Case ye, case ye on with your vizards, there 's money of the king's coming down the hill, 'tis going to the King's Exchequer.

FALSTAFF: You lie ye rogue, 'tis going to the king's Tavern.

GADSHILL: There 's enough to make us all.

FALSTAFF: To be hang'd.

PRINCE: Sirs you four shall front them in the narrow lane: Ned Poins, and I will walk lower, if they scape from your encounter, then they light on us.

PETO: How many be there of them?

GADSHILL: Some eight or ten.

FALSTAFF: 'Zounds will they not rob us?

PRINCE: What, a coward Sir John Paunch.

FALSTAFF: Indeed I am not John of Gaunt your grandfather, but yet no coward, Hal.

PRINCE: Well, we leave that to the proof.

POINS: Sirrah Jack, thy horse stands behind the hedge, when thou need'st him, there thou shalt find him: farewell and stand fast.

FALSTAFF: Now cannot I strike him if I should be hang'd.

PRINCE: Ned, where are our disguises?

POINS: Here, hard by, stand close.

FALSTAFF: Now my masters, happy man be his dole, say I, every man to his business.

Enter the Travellers.

TRAVELLER: Come neighbour, the boy shall lead our horses down the hill, we 'll walk afoot awhile and ease our legs.

THIEVES: Stand.

TRAVELLERS: Jesus bless us.

FALSTAFF: Strike, down with them, cut the villains' throats, ah whoreson caterpillars, bacon-fed knaves, they hate us youth, down with them, fleece them.

TRAVELLERS: O we are undone, both we and ours for ever.

FALSTAFF: Hang ye gorbellied knaves, are ye undone, no ye fat chuffs, I would your store were here: on bacons on, what ye knaves young men must live, you are grand jurors, are ye, we 'll jure ye 'faith.

Here they rob and bind them. Exeunt.

Enter the Prince and Poins.

PRINCE: The thieves have bound the true men, now could thou and I rob the thieves, and go merrily to London, it would be argument for a week, laughter for a month, and a good jest for ever.

POINS: Stand close, I hear them coming.

Enter the Thieves again.

FALSTAFF: Come my masters, let us share and then to horse before day, and the Prince and Poins be not two arrant cowards, there 's no equity stirring, there 's no more valour in that Poins, than in a wild-duck.

PRINCE: Your money. *As they are sharing the Prince and Poins set upon them, they all run away, and*

POINS: Villains. *Falstaff after a blow or two runs away too, leaving the booty behind them.*

PRINCE: Got with much ease. Now merrily to horse: the thieves are all scattered, and possess'd with fear so strongly, that they dare not meet each other, each takes his fellow for an officer, away good Ned, Falstaff sweats to death, and lards the lean earth as he walks along, were 't not for laughing I should pity him.

POINS: How the rogue roar'd.

Exeunt.

II. 3

Enter Hotspur solus, reading a letter.

HOTSPUR: *But for mine own part my Lord I could be well contented to be there, in respect of the love I bear your house.*
He could be contented; why is he not then? in

respect of the love he bears our house: he shows in this, he loves his own barn better than he loves our house. Let me see some more.

The purpose you undertake is dangerous,

Why that 's certain, 'tis dangerous to take a cold, to sleep, to drink, but I tell you (my Lord Fool) out of this nettle danger, we pluck this flower safety.

The purpose you undertake is dangerous, the friends you have named uncertain, the time itself unsorted, and your whole plot too light, for the counterpoise of so great an opposition.

Say you so, say you so, I say into you again, you are a shallow cowardly hind, and you lie: what a lack-brain is this? by the Lord our plot is a good plot, as ever was laid, our friends true and constant: a good plot, good friends, and full of expectation: an excellent plot, very good friends; what a frosty spirited rogue is this? why my Lord of York commends the plot, and the general course of the action. 'Zounds, and I were now by this rascal I could brain him with his Lady's fan. Is there not my father, my uncle, and myself; Lord Edmund Mortimer, my Lord of York, and Owen Glendower: is there not besides the Douglas, have I not all their letters to meet me in arms by the ninth of the next month, and are they not some of them set forward already? What a pagan rascal is this, an infidel: Ha, you shall see now in very sincerity of fear and cold heart, will he to the King, and lay open all our proceedings? O I could divide myself, and go to buffets, for moving such a dish of skim milk with so honourable an action. Hang him, let him tell the king, we are prepared: I will set forward tonight.

Enter his Lady.

How now Kate, I must leave you within these two hours.

LADY: O my good Lord, why are you thus alone?
  For what offence have I this fortnight been
  A banish'd woman from my Harry's bed?
  Tell me sweet Lord, what is 't that takes from thee
  Thy stomach, pleasure, and thy golden sleep?
  Why dost thou bend thine eyes upon the earth?
  And start so often when thou sit'st alone?
  Why hast thou lost the fresh blood in thy cheeks?
  And given my treasures and my rights of thee
  To thick ey'd musing, and curst melancholy?
  In thy faint slumbers I by thee have watch'd,
  And heard thee murmur tales of iron wars,
  Speak terms of manage to thy bounding steed,
  Cry courage to the field. And thou hast talk'd
  Of sallies and retires, of trenches, tents,
  Of palisadoes, frontiers, parapets,
  Of basilisks, of cannon, culverin,
  Of prisoners' ransom, and of soldiers slain,
  And all the currents of a heady fight,
  Thy spirit within thee hath been so at war,
  And thus hath so bestirr'd thee in thy sleep,
  That beads of sweat have stood upon thy brow
  Like bubbles in a late-disturbed stream
  And in thy face strange motions have appear'd,
  Such as we see when men restrain their breath,
  On some great sudden hest. O what portents are these?
  Some heavy business hath my Lord in hand,
  And I must know it else he loves me not.
               Enter Servant.
HOTSPUR: What ho, is Gilliams with the packet gone?
SERVANT: He is my Lord, an hour ago.
HOTSPUR: Hath Butler brought those horses from the
    Sheriff?

SERVANT: One horse my Lord he brought even now.

HOTSPUR: What horse? Roan? a cropear is it not?

SERVANT: It is my Lord.

HOTSPUR: That roan shall be my throne. Well, I will back him straight: O Esperance, bid Butler lead him forth into the park.

Exit Servant.

LADY: But hear you my Lord.

HOTSPUR: What say'st thou my Lady?

LADY: What is it carries you away?

HOTSPUR: Why, my horse (my love) my horse.

LADY: Out you mad-headed ape, a weasel hath not such a deal of spleen, as you are toss'd with. In faith I'll know your business Harry that I will. I fear my brother Mortimer doth stir about his title, and hath sent for you to line his enterprise, but if you go—

HOTSPUR: So far afoot I shall be weary love.

LADY: Come, come you paraquito, answer me directly unto this question that I ask. In faith I'll break thy little finger Harry, and if thou wilt not tell me all things true.

HOTSPUR: Away, away you trifler, love, I love thee not, I care not for thee Kate, this is no world
To play with mammets, and to tilt with lips,
We must have bloody noses, and crack'd crowns,
And pass them current too: God 's me my horse:
What say'st thou Kate? what wouldst thou have with me?

LADY: Do you not love me? do you not indeed?
Well, do not then, for since you love me not
I will not love myself. Do you not love me?
Nay tell me if you speak in jest or no.

HOTSPUR: Come, wilt thou see me ride?

And when I am a horseback I will swear
I love thee infinitely. But hark you Kate,
I must not have you henceforth question me
Whither I go, nor reason whereabout,
Whither I must, I must, and to conclude
This evening must I leave you gentle Kate,
I know you wise, but yet no farther wise
Than Harry Percy's wife, constant you are,
But yet a woman, and for secrecy
No Lady closer, for I well believe
Thou wilt not utter what thou dost not know,
And so far will I trust thee gentle Kate.

LADY: How so far.

HOTSPUR: Not an inch further, but hark you Kate,
Whither I go, thither shall you go too:
Today will I set forth, tomorrow you,
Will this content you Kate?

LADY: It must of force.

Exeunt.

II. 4

Enter Prince and Poins.

PRINCE: Ned, prithee come out of that fat room, and
lend me thy hand to laugh a little.

POINS: Where hast been Hal?

PRINCE: With three or four loggerheads, amongst three
or fourscore hogsheads. I have sounded the very base
string of humility. Sirrah, I am sworn brother to a leash
of drawers, and can call them all by their christen names,
as Tom, Dick, and Francis, they take it already upon their
salvation, that though I be but Prince of Wales, yet I am

the king of Courtesy, and tell me flatly I am no proud
Jack like Falstaff, but a Corinthian, a lad of mettle, a
good boy (by the Lord so they call me) and when I am
King of England I shall command all the good lads in
Eastcheap. They call drinking deep, dyeing scarlet, and
when you breathe in your watering they cry hem,
and bid you play it off. To conclude, I am so good a
proficient in one quarter of an hour that I can drink
with any tinker in his own language, during my life.
I tell thee Ned thou hast lost much honour, that thou wert
not with me in this action; but sweet Ned, to sweeten
which name of Ned, I give thee this pennyworth of
sugar, clapp'd even now into my hand by an underskinker, one that never spake other English in his life than
eight shillings and sixpence, and you are welcome, with
this shrill addition, anon, anon sir; score a pint of bastard
in the Half-moon, or so. But Ned, to drive away the
time till Falstaff come: I prithee do thou stand in some
by-room, while I question my puny drawer to what end
he gave me the sugar, and do thou never leave calling
Francis, that his tale to me may be nothing but anon,
step aside and I' ll show thee a present.

POINS: Francis.

PRINCE: Thou art perfect.

POINS: Francis.

Exit Poins.

Enter Drawer.

FRANCIS: Anon, anon sir. Look down into the Pomgarnet, Ralph.

PRINCE: Come hither Francis.

FRANCIS: My Lord.

PRINCE: How long hast thou to serve Francis?

FRANCIS: Forsooth, five years, and as much as to—

POINS: Francis.

FRANCIS: Anon, anon sir.

PRINCE: Five year, berlady a long lease for the clinking of pewter; but Francis, darest thou be so valiant, as to play the coward with thy Indenture, and show it a fair pair of heels, and run from it?

FRANCIS: O Lord sir, I 'll be sworn upon all the books in England, I could find in my heart.

POINS: Francis.

FRANCIS: Anon sir.

PRINCE: How old art thou Francis?

FRANCIS: Let me see, about Michaelmas next I shall be.

POINS: Francis.

FRANCIS: Anon sir, pray stay a little my Lord.

PRINCE: Nay but hark you Francis, for the sugar thou gavest me, 'twas a pennyworth, was 't not?

FRANCIS: O Lord, I would it had been two.

PRINCE: I will give thee for it a thousand pound, ask me when thou wilt, and thou shalt have it.

POINS: Francis.

FRANCIS: Anon, anon.

PRINCE: Anon Francis, no Francis, but tomorrow Francis: or Francis a Thursday; or indeed Francis when thou wilt. But Francis.

FRANCIS: My lord.

PRINCE: Wilt thou rob this leathern jerkin, crystal button, not-pated, agate ring, puke stocking, caddis garter, smooth tongue, Spanish pouch?

FRANCIS: O Lord sir, who do you mean?

PRINCE: Why then your brown bastard is your only drink: for look you Francis, your white canvas doublet will sully. In Barbary sir, it cannot come to so much.

FRANCIS: What sir?

POINS: Francis.

PRINCE: Away you rogue, dost thou not hear them call?
Here they both call him; the Drawer stands amazed,
not knowing which way to go.
Enter Vintner.

VINTNER: What stand'st thou still and hear'st such a
calling? Look to the guests within. [*Exit Francis.*]
My Lord, old Sir John with half a dozen more are at the
door, shall I let them in?

PRINCE: Let them alone awhile, and then open the door:
Poins.

POINS: Anon, anon sir.

Enter Poins.

PRINCE: Sirrah, Falstaff and the rest of the thieves are
at the door, shall we be merry?

POINS: As merry as crickets my lad, but hark ye, what
cunning match have you made with this jest of the
Drawer: come what's the issue?

PRINCE: I am now of all humours, that have showed
themselves humours since the old days of good man
Adam, to the pupil age of this present twelve a clock
at midnight. [*Enter Francis.*] What's a clock Francis?

FRANCIS: Anon, anon sir.

Exit.

PRINCE: That ever this fellow should have fewer words
than a parrot, and yet the son of a woman. His industry
is upstairs and downstairs, his eloquence the parcel of a
reckoning. I am not yet of Percy's mind, the Hotspur
of the North, he that kills me some six or seven dozen of
Scots at a breakfast: washes his hands, and says to his
wife, fie upon this quiet life, I want work. O my sweet
Harry says she! how many hast thou kill'd today?
Give my roan horse a drench (says he) and answers some

fourteen, an hour after: a trifle, a trifle. I prithee call in
Falstaff, I 'll play Percy, and that damn'd brawn shall
play Dame Mortimer his wife. *Rivo* says the drunkard:
call in Ribs, call in Tallow.

Enter Falstaff, Gadshill, Bardolph, and Peto.

POINS: Welcome Jack, where hast thou been?

FALSTAFF: A plague of all cowards I say, and a vengeance
too, marry and amen: give me a cup of sack boy.
Ere I lead this life long I 'll sew netherstocks and mend
them, and foot them too. A plague of all cowards.
Give me a cup of sack rogue, is there no virtue extant?
He drinketh.

PRINCE: Didst thou never see Titan kiss a dish of butter,
pitiful hearted Titan that melted at the sweet tale of the
sun's, if thou didst, then behold that compound.

FALSTAFF: You rogue, here 's lime in this sack too: there
is nothing but roguery to be found in villainous man,
yet a coward is worse than a cup of sack with lime
in it. A villainous coward. Go thy ways old Jack,
die when thou wilt, if manhood, good manhood be
not forgot upon the face of the earth, then am I
a shotten herring: there lives not three good men
unhang'd in England, and one of them is fat, and
grows old, God help the while, a bad world I say, I
would I were a weaver. I could sing psalms, or any thing.
A plague of all cowards I say still.

PRINCE: How now Woolsack, what mutter you?

FALSTAFF: A king's son, if I do not beat thee out of
thy kingdom with a dagger of lath, and drive all thy
subjects afore thee like a flock of wild geese, I 'll never
wear hair on my face more, you Prince of Wales.

PRINCE: Why you whoreson round-man, what 's the
matter?

FALSTAFF: Are not you a coward? answer me to that, and Poins there.

POINS: 'Zounds ye fat paunch, and ye call me coward by the Lord I'll stab thee.

FALSTAFF: I call thee coward? I'll see thee damn'd ere I call thee coward, but I would give a thousand pound I could run as fast as thou canst. You are straight enough in the shoulders, you care not who sees your back: call you that backing of your friends? a plague upon such backing, give me them that will face me, give me a cup of sack. I am a rogue if I drunk today.

PRINCE: O villain, thy lips are scarce wip'd since thou drunk'st last.

FALSTAFF: All's one for that. *He drinketh.*

A plague of all cowards still say I.

PRINCE: What's the matter?

FALSTAFF: What's the matter, there be four of us here have ta'en a thousand pound this day morning.

PRINCE: Where is it Jack, where is it?

FALSTAFF: Where is it? taken from us it is: a hundred upon poor four of us.

PRINCE: What, a hundred, man?

FALSTAFF: I am a rogue if I were not at half sword with a dozen of them two hours together. I have scap'd by miracle. I am eight times thrust through the doublet, four through the hose, my buckler cut through and through, my sword hack'd like a hand-saw, *ecce signum.* I never dealt better since I was a man, all would not do. A plague of all cowards, let them speak, if they speak more or less than truth, they are villains, and the sons of darkness.

PRINCE: Speak sirs, how was it?

GADSHILL: We four set upon some dozen.

FALSTAFF: Sixteen at least my Lord.

GADSHILL: And bound them.

PETO: No, no, they were not bound.

FALSTAFF: You rogue they were bound every man of them, or I am a Jew else: an Ebrew Jew.

GADSHILL: As we were sharing, some six or seven fresh men set upon us.

FALSTAFF: And unbound the rest, and then come in the other.

PRINCE: What, fought you with them all?

FALSTAFF: All, I know not what you call all, but if I fought not with fifty of them I am a bunch of radish: if there were not two or three and fifty upon poor old Jack, then am I no two-legg'd creature.

PRINCE: Pray God you have not murder'd some of them.

FALSTAFF: Nay, that's past praying for, I have pepper'd two of them. Two I am sure I have paid, two rogues in buckram suits: I tell thee what Hal, if I tell thee a lie, spit in my face, call me horse; thou knowest my old ward: here I lay, and thus I bore my point, four rogues in buckram let drive at me.

PRINCE: What four? thou saidst but two even now.

FALSTAFF: Four Hal, I told thee four.

POINS: Ay, ay, he said four.

FALSTAFF: These four came all a front, and mainly thrust at me, I made me no more ado, but took all their seven points in my target, thus.

PRINCE: Seven, why there were but four even now.

FALSTAFF: In buckram.

POINS: Ay four in buckram suits.

FALSTAFF: Seven by these hilts, or I am a villain else.

PRINCE: Prithee let him alone, we shall have more anon.

FALSTAFF: Dost thou hear me Hal?

PRINCE: Ay, and mark thee too Jack.

FALSTAFF: Do so, for it is worth the list'ning to, these nine in buckram that I told thee of.

PRINCE: So, two more already.

FALSTAFF: Their points being broken.

POINS: Down fell their hose.

FALSTAFF: Began to give me ground: but I followed me close, came in, foot, and hand, and with a thought, seven of the eleven I paid.

PRINCE: O monstrous! eleven buckram men grown out of two.

FALSTAFF: But as the devil would have it, three misbegotten knaves in Kendal green came at my back, and let drive at me, for it was so dark Hal, that thou couldest not see thy hand.

PRINCE: These lies are like their father that begets them, gross as a mountain, open, palpable. Why thou claybrain'd guts, thou knotty-pated fool, thou whoreson obscene greasy tallow-catch.

FALSTAFF: What art thou mad? art thou mad? is not the truth the truth?

PRINCE: Why, how couldst thou know these men in Kendal green when it was so dark thou couldst not see thy hand, come tell us your reason. What sayest thou to this?

POINS: Come your reason, Jack your reason.

FALSTAFF: What, upon compulsion? 'Zounds, and I were at the strappado, or all the racks in the world, I would not tell you on compulsion. Give you a reason on compulsion? if reasons were as plentiful as blackberries, I would give no man a reason upon compulsion, I.

PRINCE: I 'll be no longer guilty of this sin. This sanguine coward, this bed-presser, this horse-back-breaker, this huge hill of flesh.

FALSTAFF: 'Zblood you starveling, you elfskin, you dried neat's tongue, you bull's pizzle, you stockfish: O for breath to utter what is like thee, you tailor's-yard, you sheath, you bowcase, you vile standing tuck.

PRINCE: Well, breathe a while, and then to it again, and when thou hast tired thyself in base comparisons hear me speak but this.

POINS: Mark Jack.

PRINCE: We two saw you four set on four, and bound them and were masters of their wealth: mark now how a plain tale shall put you down, then did we two set on you four, and with a word, outfac'd you from your prize, and have it, yea and can show it you here in the house: and Falstaff you carried your guts away as nimbly, with as quick dexterity, and roar'd for mercy, and still run and roar'd, as ever I heard bull-calf. What a slave art thou to hack thy sword as thou hast done? and then say it was in fight. What trick? what device? what starting hole canst thou now find out, to hide thee from this open and apparent shame?

POINS: Come, let's hear Jack, what trick hast thou now?

FALSTAFF: By the Lord, I knew ye as well as he that made ye. Why hear you my masters, was it for me to kill the heir apparent? should I turn upon the true prince? why thou knowest I am as valiant as Hercules: but beware instinct, the lion will not touch the true prince, instinct is a great matter. I was now a coward on instinct, I shall think the better of myself, and thee during my life; I for a valiant lion, and thou for a true prince: but by the Lord, lads, I am glad you have the money. Hostess clap to the doors, watch tonight, pray tomorrow, gallants, lads, boys, hearts of gold, all the titles of good fellowship come to you. What shall we be merry, shall we have a play extempore?

PRINCE: Content, and the argument shall be thy running away.

FALSTAFF: Ah, no more of that Hal and thou lovest me.
Enter Hostess.

HOSTESS: O Jesu, my Lord the prince!

PRINCE: How now my lady the hostess, what sayest thou to me?

HOSTESS: Marry my Lord there is a nobleman of the court at door would speak with you: he says he comes from your father.

PRINCE: Give him as much as will make him a royal man, and send him back again to my mother.

FALSTAFF: What manner of man is he?

HOSTESS: An old man.

FALSTAFF: What doth gravity out of his bed at midnight? Shall I give him his answer?

PRINCE: Prithee do Jack.

FALSTAFF: Faith and I'll send him packing.
Exit.

PRINCE: Now sirs, birlady you fought fair, so did you Peto, so did you Bardolph, you are lions too, you ran away upon instinct, you will not touch the true prince, no fie.

BARDOLPH: Faith I ran when I saw others run.

PRINCE: Faith tell me now in earnest, how came Falstaff's sword so hack'd?

PETO: Why, he hack'd it with his dagger, and said he would swear truth out of England, but he would make you believe it was done in fight, and persuaded us to do the like.

BARDOLPH: Yea, and to tickle our noses with speargrass, to make them bleed, and then to beslubber our garments with it, and swear it was the blood of true men. I did that I did not this seven year before, I blush'd to hear his monstrous devices.

PRINCE: O villain, thou stolest a cup of sack eighteen years ago and wert taken with the manner, and ever since thou hast blush'd extempore, thou hadst fire and sword on thy side, and yet thou rann'st away, what instinct hadst thou for it?

BARDOLPH: My Lord do you see these meteors? do you behold these exhalations?

PRINCE: I do.

BARDOLPH: What think you they portend?

PRINCE: Hot livers, and cold purses.

BARDOLPH: Choler, my Lord, if rightly taken.

Enter Falstaff.

PRINCE: No if rightly taken halter. Here comes lean Jack, here comes bare bone: how now my sweet creature of bumbast, how long is 't ago Jack since thou sawest thine own knee?

FALSTAFF: My own knee? When I was about thy years (Hal) I was not an eagle's talon in the waist, I could have crept into any Alderman's thumb-ring: a plague of sighing and grief, it blows a man up like a bladder. There 's villainous news abroad, here was Sir John Bracy from your father: you must to the court in the morning. That same mad fellow of the North Percy, and he of Wales that gave Amamon the bastinado and made Lucifer cuckold, and swore the devil his true liegeman upon the cross of a Welsh hook: what a plague call you him?

POINS: O, Glendower.

FALSTAFF: Owen, Owen, the same, and his son-in-law

Mortimer, and old Northumberland, and that sprightly Scot of Scots, Douglas, that runs a horseback up a hill perpendicular.

PRINCE: He that rides at high speed, and with his pistol kills a sparrow flying.

FALSTAFF: You have hit it.

PRINCE: So did he never the sparrow.

FALSTAFF: Well, that rascal hath good mettle in him, he will not run.

PRINCE: Why, what a rascal art thou then, to praise him so for running?

FALSTAFF: A horseback (ye cuckoo) but afoot he will not budge a foot.

PRINCE: Yes Jack, upon instinct.

FALSTAFF: I grant ye upon instinct: well he is there too, and one Mordack, and a thousand blue caps more. Worcester is stol'n away tonight, thy father's beard is turn'd white with the news, you may buy land now as cheap as stinking mackrel.

PRINCE: Why then, it is like if there come a hot June, and this civil buffeting hold, we shall buy maidenheads as they buy hob nails, by the hundreds.

FALSTAFF: By the mass lad thou sayest true, it is like we shall have good trading that way: but tell me Hal, art not thou horrible afeard? thou being heir apparent, could the world pick thee out three such enemies again as that fiend Douglas, that spirit Percy, and that devil Glendower, art thou not horribly afraid? doth not thy blood thrill at it?

PRINCE: Not a whit i' faith, I lack some of thy instinct.

FALSTAFF: Well thou wilt be horribly chid tomorrow when thou comest to thy father, if thou love me practise an answer.

PRINCE: Do thou stand for my father and examine me upon the particulars of my life.

FALSTAFF: Shall I? content. This chair shall be my state, this dagger my sceptre, and this cushion my crown.

PRINCE: Thy state is taken for a join'd stool, thy golden sceptre .for a leaden dagger, and thy precious rich crown for a pitiful bald crown.

FALSTAFF:Well, and the fire of grace be not quite out of thee now shalt thou be moved. Give me a cup of sack to make my eyes look red, that it may be thought I have wept, for I must speak in passion, and I will do it in King Cambyses' vein.

PRINCE: Well, here is my leg.

FALSTAFF: And here is my speech; stand aside Nobility.

HOSTESS: O Jesu, this is excellent sport i' faith.

FALSTAFF: Weep not sweet Queen, for trickling tears are vain.

HOSTESS: O the father, how he holds his countenance!

FALSTAFF: For God's sake Lords, convey my trustful Queen,
For tears do stop the floodgates of her eyes.

HOSTESS: O Jesu, he doth it as like one of these harlotry players as ever I see.

FALSTAFF: Peace good pint-pot, peace good tickle-brain. Harry, I do not only marvel where thou spendest thy time, but also how thou art accompanied. For though the camomile, the more it is trodden on, the faster it grows: so youth the more it is wasted, the sooner it wears: that thou art my son I have partly thy mother's word, partly my own opinion, but chiefly a villainous trick of thine eye, and a foolish hanging of thy nether lip, that doth warrant me. If then thou be son to me, here lies the point, why being son to me, art thou so pointed at? shall the blessed sun of heaven prove a micher, and eat black-berries? a question not to be ask'd. Shall the son of England prove a thief, and take purses? a question to be ask'd. There is a thing Harry, which thou hast often heard of, and it is known to many in our land by the name of pitch. This pitch (as ancient writers do report) doth defile, so doth the company thou keepest: for Harry, now I do not speak to thee in drink, but in tears; not in pleasure but in passion: not in words only, but in woes also: and yet there is a virtuous man, whom I have often noted in thy company, but I know not his name.

PRINCE: What manner of man and it like your Majesty?

FALSTAFF: A goodly portly man i' faith, and a corpulent, of a cheerful look, a pleasing eye, and a most noble carriage, and as I think his age some fifty, or birlady inclining to three score, and now I remember me, his name is Falstaff, if that man should be lewdly given, he deceiveth me. For Harry, I see virtue in his looks: if then the tree may be known by the fruit, as the fruit by the tree, then peremptorily I speak it, there is virtue in that Falstaff, him keep with, the rest banish, and tell me now thou naughty varlet, tell me where hast thou been this month?

PRINCE: Dost thou speak like a king, do thou stand for me, and I 'll play my father.

FALSTAFF: Depose me, if thou dost it half so gravely, so majestically, both in word and matter, hang me up by the heels for a rabbit sucker, or a poulter's hare.

PRINCE: Well, here I am set.

FALSTAFF: And here I stand, judge my masters.

PRINCE: Now Harry, whence come you?

FALSTAFF: My noble Lord from Eastcheap.

PRINCE: The complaints I hear of thee are grievous.

FALSTAFF: 'Zblood my Lord they are false: nay I'll tickle ye for a young prince i' faith.

PRINCE: Swearest thou ungracious boy, henceforth ne'er look on me, thou art violently carried away from grace, there is a devil haunts thee in the likeness of an old fat man, a tun of man is thy companion: why dost thou converse with that trunk of humours, that boltinghutch of beastliness, that swoll'n parcel of dropsies, that huge bombard of sack, that stuff'd cloak-bag of guts, that roasted Manningtree ox with the pudding in his belly, that reverend vice, that grey iniquity, that father ruffian, that vanity in years, wherein is he good, but to taste sack and drink it? wherein neat and cleanly, but to carve a capon and eat it? wherein cunning, but in craft? wherein crafty, but in villainy? wherein villainous, but in all things? wherein worthy, but in nothing?

FALSTAFF: I would your grace would take me with you, whom means your grace?

PRINCE: That villainous abominable misleader of youth, Falstaff, that old white bearded Satan.

FALSTAFF: My Lord, the man I know.

PRINCE: I know thou dost.

FALSTAFF: But to say I know more harm in him than in myself, were to say more than I know: that he is old the more the pity, his white hairs do witness it, but that he is saving your reverence, a whoremaster, that I utterly deny: if sack and sugar be a fault, God help the wicked: if to be old and merry be a sin, then many an old host that I know is damn'd: if to be fat be to be hated, then Pharaoh's lean kine are to be loved. No my good Lord banish Peto, banish Bardolph, banish Poins, but for sweet Jack Falstaff, kind Jack Falstaff, true Jack Falstaff, valiant Jack Falstaff and therefore more valiant being as he is old Jack Falstaff, banish not him thy Harry's company, banish not him thy Harry's company, banish plump Jack, and banish all the world.

PRINCE: I do, I will.

Exeunt Hostess, Francis, and Bardolph.

Enter Bardolph, running.

BARDOLPH: O my Lord, my Lord, the Sheriff with a most monstrous watch is at the door.

FALSTAFF: Out ye rogue, play out the play, I have much to say in the behalf of that Falstaff.

Enter the Hostess.

HOSTESS: O Jesu, my Lord, my Lord!

PRINCE: Heigh, heigh, the Devil rides upon a fiddle-stick, what's the matter?

HOSTESS: The Sheriff and all the watch are at the door, they are come to search the house, shall I let them in?

FALSTAFF: Dost thou hear Hal? never call a true piece of gold a counterfeit, thou art essentially made without seeming so.

PRINCE: And thou a natural coward without instinct.

FALSTAFF: I deny your major, if you will deny the Sheriff so, if not, let him enter. If I become not a cart as well as another man, a plague on my bringing up, I hope I shall as soon be strangled with a halter as another.

PRINCE: Go hide thee behind the arras, the rest walk up above, now my masters for a true face, and good conscience.

FALSTAFF: Both which I have had, but their date is out, and therefore I 'll hide me.

PRINCE: Call in the Sheriff.

Exeunt all except the Prince and Peto.

Enter Sheriff and the Carrier.

Now master Sheriff, what is your will with me?

SHERIFF: First pardon me my Lord. A hue and cry hath followed certain men unto this house.

PRINCE: What men?

SHERIFF: One of them is well known my gracious Lord, a gross fat man.

CARRIER: As fat as butter.

PRINCE: The man I do assure you is not here,
For I myself at this time have employ'd him:
And Sheriff, I will engage my word to thee,
That I will by tomorrow dinner time
Send him to answer thee or any man,
For anything he shall be charg'd withal,
And so let me entreat you leave the house.

SHERIFF: I will my Lord: there are two gentlemen
Have in this robbery lost three hundred marks.

PRINCE: It may be so: if he have robb'd these men
He shall be answerable, and so farewell.

SHERIFF: Good night my noble Lord.

PRINCE: I think it is good morrow is it not?

SHERIFF: Indeed my Lord, I think it be two a clock.

Exeunt Sheriff and Carrier.

PRINCE: This oily rascal is known as well as Paul's: go call him forth.

PETO: Falstaff: fast asleep behind the arras, and snorting like a horse.

PRINCE: Hark how hard he fetches breath, search his pockets. [*He searcheth his pockets, and findeth certain papers.*] What hast thou found?

PETO: Nothing but papers my Lord.

PRINCE: Let's see what they be, read them.

Item a capon   .   .   .   2*s.*   2*d.*

Item sauce   .   .   .   .   4*d.*
Item sack two gallons   .   .   5*s.*   8*d.*
Item anchovies and sack after
    supper   .   .   .   .   2*s.*   6*d.*
Item bread   .   .   .   ob.

PRINCE: O monstrous! but one halfpennyworth of bread to this intolerable deal of sack? what there is else keep close, we 'll read it at more advantage; there let him sleep till day, I 'll to the court in the morning. We must all to the wars, and thy place shall be honourable. I 'll procure this fat rogue a charge of foot, and I know his death will be a march of twelve score, the money shall be paid back again with advantage; be with me betimes in the morning, and so good morrow Peto.

PETO: Good morrow good my Lord.

Exeunt.

III. I

Enter Hotspur, Worcester, Lord Mortimer, Owen
Glendower.

MORTIMER: These promises are fair, the parties sure,
    And our induction full of prosperous hope.

HOTSPUR: Lord Mortimer, and cousin Glendower will you sit down? and Uncle Worcester; a plague upon it I have forgot the map.

GLENDOWER: No here it is; sit Couisn Percy, sit good Cousin Hotspur, for by that name as oft as Lancaster doth speak of you, his cheek looks pale, and with a rising sigh he wisheth you in heaven.

HOTSPUR: And you in hell, as oft as he hears Owen Glendower spoke of.

GLENDOWER: I cannot blame him: at my nativity
    The front of heaven was full of fiery shapes

Of burning cressets, and at my birth
The frame and huge foundation of the earth
Shaked like a coward.

HOTSPUR: Why so it would have done at the same season
if your mother's cat had but kitten'd, though yourself
had never been born.

GLENDOWER: I say the earth did shake when I was born.

HOTSPUR: And I say the earth was not of my mind,
If you suppose as fearing you it shook.

GLENDOWER: The heavens were all on fire, the earth
did tremble.

HOTSPUR: Oh then the earth shook to see the heavens
on fire,
And not in fear of your nativity,
Diseased nature oftentimes breaks forth
In strange eruptions, oft the teeming earth
Is with a kind of colic pinch'd and vex'd,
By the imprisoning of unruly wind
Within her womb, which for enlargement striving
Shakes the old Beldam earth, and topples down
Steeples and mossgrown towers. At your birth
Our Grandam earth, having this distemp'rature
In passion shook,

GLENDOWER: Cousin of many men
I do not bear these crossings, give me leave
To tell you once again that at my birth
The front of heaven was full of fiery shapes,
The goats ran from the mountains, and the herds
Were strangely clamorous to the frighted fields.
These signs have mark'd me extraordinary,
And all the courses of my life do show
I am not in the roll of common men:
Where is he living clipp'd in with the sea,

That chides the banks of England, Scotland, Wales,
Which calls me pupil or hath read to me?
And bring him out that is but woman's son
Can trace me in the tedious ways of Art,
And hold me pace in deep experiments.

HOTSPUR: I think there 's no man speaks better Welsh:
I 'll to dinner.

MORTIMER: Peace cousin Percy, you will make him mad.

GLENDOWER: I can call spirits from the vasty deep.

HOTSPUR: Why so can I, or so can any man,
But will they come when you do call for them?

GLENDOWER: Why I can teach you cousin to command
the Devil.

HOTSPUR: And I can teach thee coz to shame the devil,
By telling truth. Tell truth and shame the devil:
If thou have power to raise him bring him hither,
And I 'll be sworn I have power to shame him hence:
Oh while you live tell truth and shame the devil.

MORTIMER: Come, come, no more of this unprofitable
chat.

GLENDOWER: Three times hath Henry Bolingbroke
made head
Against my power, thrice from the banks of Wye,
And sandy bottom'd Severn have I sent him
Bootless home, and weatherbeaten back.

HOTSPUR: Home without boots, and in foul weather too,
How 'scapes he agues in the devil's name?

GLENDOWER: Come here is the map, shall we divide our
right,
According to our threefold order ta'en?

MORTIMER: The Archdeacon hath divided it
Into three limits very equally:
England from Trent, and Severn hitherto,

By South and East is to my part assign'd:
All westward, Wales beyond the Severn shore,
And all the fertile land within that bound
To Owen Glendower: and dear coz to you
The remnant northward lying off from Trent,
And our indentures tripartite are drawn,
Which being sealed interchangeably,
(A business that this night may execute:)
Tomorrow cousin Percy you and I
And my good Lord of Worcester will set forth
To meet your father and the Scottish power,
As is appointed us at Shrewsbury.
My father Glendower is not ready yet,
Nor shall we need his help these fourteen days,
Within that space you may have drawn together
Your tenants, friends, and neighbouring gentlemen.

GLENDOWER: A shorter time shall send me to you Lords,
And in my conduct shall your Ladies come,
From whom you now must steal and take no leave,
For there will be a world of water shed,
Upon the parting of your wives and you.

HOTSPUR: Methinks my moiety North from Burton here,
In quantity equals not one of yours,
See how this river comes me cranking in,
And cuts me from the best of all my land,
A huge half moon, a monstrous cantle out,
I 'll have the current in this place damm'd up,
And here the smug and silver Trent shall run
In a new channel fair and evenly,
It shall not wind with such a deep indent,
To rob me of so rich a bottom here

GLENDOWER: Not wind it shall, it must, you see it doth.

MORTIMER: Yea, but mark how he bears his course, and

runs me up with like advantage on the other side,
gelding the opposed continent as much as on the other
side it takes from you.

WORCESTER: Yea but a little charge will trench him here,
And on this north side win this cape of land,
And then he runs straight and even.

HOTSPUR: I 'll have it so a little charge will do it.

GLENDOWER: I 'll not have it alter'd.

HOTSPUR: Will not you?

GLENDOWER: No nor you shall not.

HOTSPUR: Who shall say me nay?

GLENDOWER: Why that will I.

HOTSPUR: Let me not understand you then, speak it in
Welsh.

GLENDOWER: I can speak English Lord as well as you,
For I was train'd up in the English court,
Where being but young I framed to the harp
Many an English ditty lovely well,
And gave the tongue a helpful ornament,
A virtue that was never seen in you.

HOTSPUR: Marry and I am glad of it with all my heart,
I had rather be a kitten and cry mew,
Than one of these same metre ballad mongers,
I had rather hear a brazen canstick turn'd
Or a dry wheel grate on the axle tree,
And that would set my teeth nothing on edge,
Nothing so much as mincing poetry,
'Tis like the forc'd gait of a shuffling nag.

GLENDOWER: Come, you shall have Trent turn'd.

HPTSPUR: I do not care, I 'll give thrice so much land
To any well deserving friend:
But in the way of bargain mark ye me,
I 'll cavil on the ninth part of a hair,

Are the indentures drawn, shall we be gone?

GLENDOWER: The moon shines fair, you may away by
    night:
I 'll haste the writer, and withal
Break with your wives of your departure hence,
I am afraid my daughter will run mad,
So much she doteth on her Mortimer.

Exit.

MORTIMER: Fie cousin Percy, how you cross my father.

HOTSPUR: I cannot choose, sometime he angers me
With telling me of the Moldwarp and the Ant,
Of the dreamer Merlin and his prophecies,
And of a Dragon and a finless fish,
A clip-wing'd Griffin and a moulten raven,
A couching Lion and a ramping Cat,
And such a deal of skimble skamble stuff,
As puts me from my faith. I tell you what,
He held me last night at least nine hours
In reckoning up the several Devils' names
That were his lackeys, I cried hum, and well go to,
But mark'd him not a word. O he is as tedious
As a tired horse, a railing wife,
Worse than a smoky house. I had rather live
With cheese and garlic in a windmill far,
Then feed on cates and have him talk to me,
In any summer house in Christendom.

MORTIMER: In faith he is a worthy gentleman,
Exceedingly well read and profited
In strange concealments, valiant as a lion,
And wondrous affable; and as bountiful
As mines of India; shall I tell you cousin,
He holds your temper in a high respect
And curbs himself even of his natural scope,

When you come 'cross his humour, faith he does,
I warrant you that man is not alive
Might so have tempted him as you have done,
Without the taste of danger and reproof,
But do not use it oft, let me entreat you.

WORCESTER: In faith my Lord you are too wilful blame,
And since your coming hither have done enough
To put him quite besides his patience.
You must needs learn Lord to amend this fault,
Though sometimes it show greatness, courage, blood,
And that 's the dearest grace it renders you,
Yet oftentimes it doth present harsh rage,
Defect of manners, want of government,
Pride, haughtiness, opinion, and disdain,
The least of which haunting a nobleman,
Loseth men's hearts and leaves behind a stain
Upon the beauty of all parts besides,
Beguiling them of commendation.

HOTSPUR: Well I am school'd good manners be your
    speed,
Here come our wives, and let us take our leave.
    Enter Glendower with the Ladies.

MORTIMER: This is the deadly spite that angers me,
My wife can speak no English, I no Welsh.

GLENDOWER: My daughter weeps, she 'll not part with
    you,
She 'll be a soldier too, she 'll to the wars.

MORTIMER: Good father tell her, that she and my Aunt
    Percy
Shall follow in your conduct speedily.
    *Glendower speaks to her in Welsh, and she answers
        him in the same.*

GLENDOWER: She is desperate here,

A peevish self-will'd harlotry, one that no persuasion
can do good upon.
                    The Lady speaks in Welsh.
MORTIMER: I understand thy looks, that pretty Welsh,
     Which thou pour'st down from these swelling heavens,
     I am too perfect in, and but for shame
     In such a parley should I answer thee.
                    The Lady again in Welsh.
     I understand thy kisses, and thou mine,
     And that's a feeling disputation,
     But I will never be a truant love,
     Till I have learn'd thy language, for thy tongue
     Makes Welsh as sweet as ditties highly penn'd,
     Sung by a fair Queen in a summer's bower,
     With ravishing division to her lute.
GLENDOWER: Nay, if you melt, then will she run mad.
                    The Lady speaks again in Welsh.
MORTIMER: O I am ignorance itself in this.
GLENDOWER: She bids you on the wanton rushes lay you
     down,
     And rest your gentle head upon her lap.
     And she will sing the song that pleaseth you,
     And on your eyelids crown the God of sleep,
     Charming your blood with pleasing heaviness,
     Making such difference 'twixt wake and sleep,
     As is the difference betwixt day and night,
     The hour before the heavenly harness'd team
     Begins his golden progress in the east.
MORTIMER: With all my heart I'll sit and hear her sing,
     By that time will our book I think be drawn.
GLENDOWER: Do so, and those musicians that shall play
     to you,
     Hang in the air a thousand leagues from hence,

And straight they shall be here, sit and attend.

HOTSPUR: Come Kate, thou art perfect in lying down, come quick, quick, that I may lay my head in thy lap.

LADY PERCY: Go ye giddy goose.

The music plays.

HOTSPUR: Now I perceive the devil understands Welsh,
And 'tis no marvel he is so humorous,
Birlady he is a good musician.

LADY PERCY: Then should you be nothing but musical, for you are altogether govern'd by humours, lie still ye thief, and hear the Lady sing in Welsh.

HOTSPUR: I had rather hear Lady my brach howl in Irish.

LADY PERCY: Wouldst thou have thy head broken?

HOTSPUR: No.

LADY PERCY: Then be still.

HOTSPUR: Neither, 'tis a woman's fault.

LADY PERCY: Now God help thee.

HOTSPUR: To the Welsh Lady's bed.

LADY PERCY: What's that?

HOTSPUR: Peace, she sings.

Here the Lady sings a Welsh song.

HOTSPUR: Come Kate, I'll have your song too.

LADY PERCY: Not mine in good sooth.

HOTSPUR: Not yours in good sooth. Heart, you swear like a comfit-maker's wife, not you in good sooth, and as true as I live, and as God shall mend me, and as sure as day:
And givest such sarcenet surety for thy oaths,
As if thou never walk'st further than Finsbury.
Swear me Kate like a lady as thou art,
A good mouthfilling oath, and leave in sooth,
And such protest of pepper gingerbread
To velvet guards, and Sunday Citizens.

Come sing.

LADY PERCY: I will not sing.

HOTSPUR: 'Tis the next way to turn tailor, or be redbreast
teacher, and the indentures be drawn I 'll away within
these two hours, and so come in when ye will.

Exit.

GLENDOWER: Come, come, Lord Mortimer, you are as
slow,

As hot Lord Percy is on fire to go:

By this our book is drawn, we'll but seal,

And then to horse immediately.

MORTIMER: With all my heart.

Exeunt.

III. 2

Enter the King, Prince of Wales, and others.

KING: Lords give us leave, the Prince of Wales and I,

Must have some private conference, but be near at hand,

For we shall presently have need of you.

Exeunt Lords.

I know not whether God will have it so

For some displeasing service I have done,

That in his secret doom out of my blood,

He 'll breed revengement and a scourge for me:

But thou dost in thy passages of life,

Make me believe that thou art only mark'd

For the hot vengeance, and the rod of heaven,

To punish my mistreadings. Tell me else

Could such inordinate and low desires,

Such poor, such bare, such lewd, such mean attempts,

Such barren pleasures, rude society

As thou art match'd withal, and grafted to,

Accompany the greatness of thy blood,
And hold their level with thy princely heart?
PRINCE: So please your Majesty, I would I could
Quit all offences with as clear excuse,
As well as I am doubtless I can purge
Myself of many I am charg'd withal,
Yet such extenuation let me beg,
As in reproof of many tales devis'd,
Which oft the ear of greatness needs must hear
By smiling pickthanks, and base newsmongers,
I may for some things true, wherein my youth
Hath faulty wander'd, and irregular,
Find pardon on my true submission.
KING: God pardon thee, yet let me wonder, Harry,
At thy affections, which do hold a wing
Quite from the flight of all thy ancestors,
Thy place in council thou hast rudely lost
Which by thy younger brother is supplied,
And art almost an alien to the hearts
Of all the Court and princes of my blood,
The hope and expectation of thy time
Is ruin'd, and the soul of every man
Prophetically do forethink thy fall:
Had I so lavish of my presence been,
So common hackney'd in the eyes of men,
So stale and cheap to vulgar company,
Opinion that did help me to the crown,
Had still kept loyal to possession,
And left me in reputeless banishment,
A fellow of no mark nor likelihood.
By being seldom seen, I could not stir
But like a Comet I was wonder'd at;
That men would tell their children this is he:

Others would say, where, which is Bolingbroke?
And then I stole all courtesy from heaven,
And dress'd myself in such humility
That I did pluck allegiance from men's hearts,
Loud shouts, and salutations from their mouths,
Even in the presence of the crowned king.
Thus did I keep my person fresh and new,
My presence like a robe pontifical,
Ne'er seen but wonder'd at and so my state
Seldom, but sumptuous show'd like a feast,
And won by rareness such solemnity.
The skipping king, he ambled up and down,
With shallow jesters, and rash bavin wits,
Soon kindled, and soon burnt, carded his state,
Mingled his royalty with cap'ring fools,
Had his great name profaned with their scorns,
And gave his countenance against his name
To laugh at gibing boys, and stand the push
Of every beardless vain comparative,
Grew a companion to the common streets,
Enfeoff'd himself to popularity,
That being daily swallowed by men's eyes,
They surfeited with honey, and began
To loathe the taste of sweetness whereof a little
More than a little, is by much too much.
So when he had occasion to be seen,
He was but as the Cuckoo is in June,
Heard, not regarded: Seen, but with such eyes
As sick and blunted with community,
Afford no extraordinary gaze,
Such as is bent on sun-like majesty,
When it shines seldom in admiring eyes,
But rather drowz'd, and hung their eyelids down,

Slept in his face, and render'd such aspect
As cloudy men use to their adversaries
Being with his presence glutted, gorg'd, and full,
And in that very line Harry standest thou,
For thou hast lost thy princely privilege
With vile participation. Not an eye
But is aweary of thy common sight,
Save mine, which hath desired to see thee more,
Which now doth that I would not have it do,
Make blind itself with foolish tenderness.

PRINCE: I shall hereafter my thrice gracious Lord,
Be more myself.

KING: For all the world,
As thou art to this hour was Richard then,
When I from France set foot at Ravenspurgh,
And even as I was then, is Percy now,
Now by my sceptre, and my soul to boot,
He hath more worthy interest to the state
Than thou the shadow of succession.
For of no right, nor colour like to right,
He doth fill fields with harness in the realm,
Turns head against the lion's armed jaws,
And being no more in debt to years than thou,
Leads ancient Lords, and reverend Bishops on
To bloody battles, and to bruising arms.
What never dying honour hath he got
Against renowned Douglas? Whose high deeds,
Whose hot incursions, and great name in arms,
Holds from all soldiers chief majority
And military title capital
Through all the kingdoms that acknowledge Christ.
Thrice hath this Hotspur Mars in swathling clothes,
This infant warrior in his enterprizes,

Discomfited great Douglas, ta'en him once,
Enlarg'd him, and made a friend of him,
To fill the mouth of deep defiance up,
And shake the peace and safety of our throne,
And what say you to this? Percy, Northumberland,
The Archbishop's grace of York, Douglas, Mortimer,
Capitulate against us, and are up
But wherefore do I tell these news to thee?
Why Harry do I tell thee of my foes,
Which art my nearest and dearest enemy?
Thou that art like enough through vassal fear,
Base inclination, and the start of spleen,
To fight against me under Percy's pay,
To dog his heels, and curtsy at his frowns,
To show how much thou art degenerate.
PRINCE: Do not think so, you shall not find it so,
And God forgive them that so much have sway'd
Your majesty's good thoughts away from me.
I will redeem all this on Percy's head,
And in the closing of some glorious day
Be bold to tell you that I am your son,
When I will wear a garment all of blood,
And stain my favours in a bloody mask,
Which wash'd away shall scour my shame with it,
And that shall be the day whene'er it lights,
That this same child of honour and renown,
This gallant Hotspur, this all praised knight,
And your unthought of Harry chance to meet,
For every honour sitting on his helm
Would they were multitudes, and on my head
My shames redoubled. For the time will come
That I shall make this Northern youth exchange
His glorious deeds for my indignities.

Percy is but my factor, good my Lord,
To engross up glorious deeds on my behalf.
And I will call him to so strict account,
That he shall render every glory up,
Yea, even the slightest worship of his time,
Or I will tear the reckoning from his heart.
This in the name of God I promise here,
The which if he be pleas'd I shall perform:
I do beseech your majesty may salve
The long grown wounds of my intemperance,
If not, the end of life cancels all bands,
And I will die a hundred thousand deaths
Ere break the smallest parcel of this vow.

KING: A hundred thousand rebels die in this,
Thou shalt have charge and sovereign trust herein.
How now good Blunt thy looks are full of speed.

Enter Blunt.

BLUNT: So hath the business that I come to speak of.
Lord Mortimer of Scotland hath sent word,
That Douglas and the English Rebels met
The eleventh of this month at Shrewsbury,
A mighty and a fearful head they are,
If promises be kept on every hand,
As ever offer'd foul play in a state.

KING: The Earl of Westmoreland set forth today,
With him my son Lord John of Lancaster,
For this advertisement is five days old.
On Wednesday next, Harry you shall set forward,
On Thursday we ourselves will march. Our meeting
Is Bridgenorth, and Harry, you shall march
Through Gloucestershire, by which account
Our business valued some twelve days hence,
Our general forces at Bridgenorth shall meet:

Our hands are full of business, let 's away,
Advantage feeds him fat while men delay.
Exeunt.

III. 3

Enter Falstaff and Bardolph.

FALSTAFF: Bardolph, am I not fallen away vilely since
this last action? do I not bate? do I not dwindle? Why,
my skin hangs about me like an old Lady's loose gown.
I am withered like an old apple John. Well, I 'll repent
and that suddenly, while I am in some liking, I shall be
out of heart shortly, and then I shall have no strength to
repent. And I have not forgotten what the inside of a
church is made of, I am a peppercorn, a brewer's horse,
the inside of a church. Company, villainous company,
hath been the spoil of me.

BARDOLPH: Sir John, you are so fretful you cannot live
long.

FALSTAFF: Why, there is it: come sing me a bawdy
song, make me merry. I was as virtuously given as a
gentleman need to be, virtuous enough, swore little,
dic'd not above seven times a week, went to a bawdy
house not above once in a quarter of an hour, paid
money that I borrowed three or four times, lived well,
and in good compass, and now I live out of all order,
out of all compass.

BARDOLPH: Why, you are so fat, Sir John, that you
must needs be out of all compass: out of all reasonable
compass, Sir John.

FALSTAFF: Do thou amend thy face, and I 'll amend my
life: thou art our Admiral, thou bearest the lantern in

the poop, but 'tis in the nose of thee: thou art the knight of the burning lamp.

BARDOLPH: Why, Sir John, my face does you no harm.

FALSTAFF: No I 'll be sworn, I make as good use of it as many a man doth of a death's head, or a *memento mori*. I never see thy face, but I think upon hell fire, and Dives that lived in purple: for there he is in his robes burning burning. If thou wert any way given to virtue, I would swear by the face: my oath should be by this fire that God 's Angel. But thou art altogether given over: and wert indeed but for the light in thy face, the son of utter darkness. When thou rann'st up Gadshill in the night to catch my horse, if I did not think thou hadst been an *ignis fatuus*, or a ball of wildfire, there 's no purchase in money. O thou art a perpetual triumph, an everlasting bonfire light, thou hast saved me a thousand marks in links, and torches, walking with thee in the night betwixt tavern and tavern; but the sack that thou hast drunk me, would have bought me lights as good cheap, at the dearest chandler's in Europe. I have maintained that salamander of yours with fire any time this two and thirty years, God reward me for it.

BARDOLPH: 'Zblood, I would my face were in your belly.

FALSTAFF: God-a-mercy, so should I be sure to be heartburn'd. How now Dame Partlet the hen, have you inquir'd yet who pick'd my pocket?

Enter Hostess.

HOSTESS: Why Sir John, what do you think Sir John, do you think I keep thieves in my house, I have search'd, I have inquired, so has my husband, man by man, boy by boy, servant by servant, the tithe of a hair, was never lost in my house before.

FALSTAFF: Ye lie Hostess, Bardolph was shav'd, and

lost many a hair, and I 'll be sworn my pocket was pick'd: go to, you are a woman, go.

HOSTESS: Who I. No, I defy thee: God's light I was never call'd so in mine own house before.

FALSTAFF: Go to, I know you well enough.

HOSTESS: No, Sir John you do not know me, Sir John, I know you Sir John, you owe me money Sir John, and now you pick a quarrel to beguile me of it, I bought you a dozen of shirts to your back.

FALSTAFF: Dowlas, filthy dowlas. I have given them away to baker's wives, and they have made bolters of them.

HOSTESS: Now as I am a true woman, holland of eight shillings an ell, you owe money here, besides Sir John, for your diet, and by-drinkings, and money lent you four and twenty pound.

FALSTAFF: He had his part of it, let him pay.

HOSTESS: He, alas he is poor, he hath nothing.

FALSTAFF: How? poor? look upon his face. What call you rich? let them coin his nose, let them coin his cheeks, I 'll not pay a denier: what will you make a younker of me? shall I not take mine ease in mine Inn, but I shall have my pocket pick'd? I have lost a seal ring of my grandfather's worth forty mark.

HOSTESS: O Jesu, I have heard the Prince tell him I know not how oft, that that ring was copper.

FALSTAFF: How? the Prince is a Jack, a sneak-cup, 'zblood and he were here, I would cudgel him like a dog if he would say so.

Enter the Prince and Peto marching, and Falstaff meets them playing on his truncheon like a fife.

How now lad, is the wind in that door i' faith, must we all march?

BARDOLPH: Yea, two, and two, Newgate fashion.

HOSTESS: My Lord, I pray you hear me.

PRINCE: What sayest thou Mistress Quickly, how doth thy husband? I love him well, he is an honest man.

HOSTESS: Good my Lord hear me.

FALSTAFF: Prithee let her alone, and list to me.

PRINCE: What sayest thou Jack?

FALSTAFF: The other night I fell asleep here, behind the arras, and had my pocket pick'd, this house is turn'd bawdy house, they pick pockets.

PRINCE: What didst thou lose Jack?

FALSTAFF: Wilt thou believe me Hal, three or four bonds of forty pound a piece, and a seal ring of my grand-father's.

PRINCE: A trifle, some eight penny matter.

HOSTESS: So I told him my Lord, and I said I heard your grace say so: and my Lord he speaks most vilely of you, like a foul mouth'd man as he is, and said he would cudgel you.

PRINCE: What he did not?

HOSTESS: There 's neither faith, truth, nor womanhood in me else.

FALSTAFF: There 's no more faith in thee than in a stewed prune, nor no more truth in thee than in a drawn fox, and for womanhood Maid Marian may be the deputy's wife of the ward to thee. Go you thing, go.

HOSTESS: Say what thing, what thing?

FALSTAFF: What thing? why a thing to thank God on.

HOSTESS: I am no thing to thank God on, I would thou shouldst know it, I am an honest man's wife, and setting thy knighthood aside, thou art a knave to call me so.

FALSTAFF: Setting thy womanhood aside, thou art a beast to say otherwise.

HOSTESS: Say, what beast, thou knave thou?

FALSTAFF: What beast? why an otter.

PRINCE: An otter Sir John, why an otter?

FALSTAFF: Why? she 's neither fish nor flesh, a man knows not where to have her.

HOSTESS: Thou art an unjust man in saying so, thou or any man knows where to have me, thou knave thou.

PRINCE: Thou sayest true hostess, and he slanders thee most grossly.

HOSTESS: So he doth you my Lord, and said this other day you ought him a thousand pound.

PRINCE: Sirrah, do I owe you a thousand pound?

FALSTAFF: A thousand pound Hal? a million, thy love is worth a million, thou owest me thy love.

HOSTESS: Nay my Lord, he call'd you Jack, and said he would cudgel you.

FALSTAFF: Did I Bardolph?

BARDOLPH: Indeed Sir John you said so.

FALSTAFF: Yea, if he said my ring was copper.

PRINCE: I say 'tis copper, darest thou be as good as thy word now?

FALSTAFF: Why Hal? Thou knowest as thou art but man I dare, but as thou art prince, I fear thee as I fear the roaring of the lion's whelp.

PRINCE: And why not as the lion?

FALSTAFF: The king himself is to be feared as the lion, dost thou think I 'll fear thee as I fear thy father? nay and I do, I pray God my girdle break.

PRINCE: O, if it should, how would thy guts fall about thy knees? but sirrah, there 's no room for faith, truth, nor honesty, in this bosom of thine. It is all fill'd up with guts, and midriff. Charge an honest woman with picking thy pocket, why thou whoreson impudent emboss'd rascal, if there were anything in thy pocket but tavern reckonings, memorandums of bawdy houses, and one poor pennyworth of sugar-candy to make thee long winded, if thy pocket were enrich'd with any other injuries but these; I am a villain, and yet you will stand to it, you will not pocket up wrong, art thou not ashamed?

FALSTAFF: Dost thou hear Hal, thou knowest in the state of innocency Adam fell, and what should poor Jack Falstaff do in the days of villainy? thou seest I have more flesh than another man, and therefore more frailty. You confess then you pick'd my pocket?

PRINCE: It appears so by the story.

FALSTAFF: Hostess, I forgive thee, go make ready breakfast, love thy husband, look to thy servants, cherish thy guests, thou shalt find me tractable to any honest reason, thou seest I am pacified still, nay prithee be gone.

Exit Hostess.

Now Hal, to the news at court for the robbery lad, how is that answered?

PRINCE: O my sweet beef, I must still be good angel to thee, the money is paid back again.

FALSTAFF: O I do not like that paying back, 'tis a double labour.

PRINCE: I am good friends with my father and may do any thing.

FALSTAFF: Rob me the exchequer the first thing thou doest, and do it with unwash'd hands too.

BARDOLPH: Do my Lord.

PRINCE: I have procured thee Jack a charge of foot.

FALSTAFF: I would it had been of horse. Where shall I find one that can steal well, O for a fine thief of the age of two and twenty or thereabouts: I am heinously

unprovided. Well, God be thanked for these rebels, they
offend none but the virtuous; I laud them, I praise them.

PRINCE: Bardolph.

BARDOLPH: My Lord.

PRINCE: Go bear this letter to Lord John of Lancaster,
to my brother John, this to my Lord of Westmoreland. Go Peto to horse, to horse, for thou and I have
thirty miles to ride yet ere dinner time. Jack, meet me
tomorrow in the Temple hall at two o'clock in the
afternoon,
There shalt thou know thy charge, and there receive
Money and order for their furniture,
The land is burning, Percy stands on high,
And either we or they must lower lie.

FALSTAFF: Rare words, brave world: hostess, my breakfast come,
Oh I could wish this tavern were my drum.

Exit.

IV. 1

Enter Harry Hotspur, Worcester, and Douglas.

HOTSPUR: Well said my noble Scot, if speaking truth
In this fine age were not thought flattery,
Such attribution should the Douglas have,
As not a soldier of this season's stamp,
Should go so general current through the world.
By God, I cannot flatter, I do defy
The tongues of soothers, but a braver place
In my heart's love hath no man than yourself,
Nay task me to my word, approve me Lord.

DOUGLAS: Thou art the King of honour,
No man so potent breathes upon the ground,

But I will beard him.

Enter one with letters.

HOTSPUR: Do so, and 'tis well. What letters hast thou
there? I can but thank you.

MESSENGER: These letters come from your father.

HOTSPUR: Letter from him, why comes he not himself?

MESSENGER: He cannot come my lord, he is grievous sick.

HOTSPUR: 'Zounds, how has he the leisure to be sick
In such a justling time, who leads his power?
Under whose government come they along?

MESSENGER: His letters bears his mind, not I my Lord.

WORCESTER: I prithee tell me, doth he keep his bed?

MESSENGER: He did my Lord, four days ere I set forth,
And at the time of my departure thence,
He was much fear'd by his Physicians.

WORCESTER: I would the state of time had first been
whole,
Ere he by sickness had been visited,
His health was never better worth than now.

HOTSPUR: Sick now, droop now, this sickness doth infect
The very life-blood of our enterprise,
'Tis catching hither even to our camp.
He writes me here that inward sickness,
And that his friends by deputation
Could not so soon be drawn, nor did he think it meet
To lay so dangerous and dear a trust
On any soul remov'd but on his own,
Yet doth he give us bold advertisement,
That with our small conjunction we should on,
To see how fortune is dispos'd to us,
For as he writes there is no quailing now,
Because the king is certainly possess'd
Of all our purposes, what say you to it?

WORCESTER: Your father's sickness is a maim to us.
HOTSPUR: A perilous gash, a very limb lopp'd off,
  And yet in faith it is not, his present want
  Seems more than we shall find it: were it good
  To set the exact wealth of all our states
  All at one cast? to set so rich a main
  On the nice hazard of one doubtful hour?
  It were not good for therein should we read
  The very bottom and the soul of hope,
  The very list, the very utmost bound
  Of all our fortunes.
DOUGLAS: Faith, and so we should,
  Where now remains a sweet reversion,
  We may boldly spend upon the hope of what is to come
    in,
  A comfort of retirement lives in this.
HOTSPUR: A rendezvous, a home to fly unto
  If that the Devil and mischance look big
  Upon the maidenhead of our affairs.
WORCESTER: But yet I would your father had been here:
  The quality and hair of our attempt
  Brooks no division, it will be thought
  By some that know not why he is away,
  That wisdom, loyalty, and mere dislike
  Of our proceedings kept the Earl from hence,
  And think how such an apprehension
  May turn the tide of fearful faction,
  And breed a kind of question in our cause:
  For well you know we of the off'ring side
  Must keep aloof from strict arbitrement,
  And stop all sight-holes every loop from whence
  The eye of reason may pry in upon us,
  This absence of your father's draws a curtain

That shows the ignorant a kind of fear
Before not dreamt of.

HOTSPUR: You strain too far.
I rather of his absence make this use,
It lends a lustre and more great opinion,
A larger dare to our great enterprise
Than if the Earl were here, for men must think
If we without his help can make a head
To push against a kingdom, with his help
We shall o'erturn it topsy turvy down,
Yet all goes well, yet all our joints are whole.

DOUGLAS: As heart can think, there is not such a word
Spoke of in Scotland as this term of fear.

Enter Sir Richard Vernon.

HOTSPUR: My cousin Vernon, welcome by my soul.

VERNON: Pray God my news be worth a welcome lord.
The Earl of Westmoreland seven thousand strong
Is marching hitherwards, with him Prince John.

HOTSPUR: No harm, what more?

VERNON: And further I have learn'd,
The King himself in person is set forth,
Or hitherwards intended speedily
With strong and mighty preparation.

HOTSPUR: He shall be welcome too: where is his son?
The nimble footed madcap Prince of Wales,
And his comrades that daff'd the word aside
And bid it pass?

VERNON: All furnish'd all in arms:
All plum'd like estridges that with the wind
Baited like eagles having lately bath'd,
Glittering in golden coats like images,
As full of spirit as the month of May,
And gorgeous as the sun at midsummer:

Wanton as youthful goats, wild as young bulls.
I saw young Harry with his beaver on,
His cuisses on his thighs gallantly arm'd,
Rise from the ground like feathered Mercury,
And vaulted with such ease into his seat,
As if an Angel dropp'd down from the clouds,
To turn and wind a fiery Pegasus,
And witch the world with noble horsemanship.

HOTSPUR: No more, no more, worse than the sun in
    March,
This praise doth nourish agues, let them come,
They come like sacrifices in their trim,
And to the fire-ey'd maid of smoky war,
All hot and bleeding will we offer them,
The mailed Mars shall on his altar sit
Up to the ears in blood. I am on fire
To hear this rich reprisal is so nigh,
And yet not ours: Come let me taste my horse,
Who is to bear me like a thunderbolt,
Against the bosom of the Prince of Wales,
Harry to Harry shall hot horse to horse,
Meet and ne'er part till one drop down a corse:
Oh that Glendower were come.

VERNON: There is more news,
I learn'd in Worcester, as I rode along,
He cannot draw his power this fourteen days.

DOUGLAS: That's the worst tidings that I hear of yet.

WORCESTER: Ay by my faith, that bears a frosty sound.

HOTSPUR: What may the king's whole battle reach unto?

VERNON: To thirty thousand.

HOTSPUR: Forty let it be,
My father and Glendower being both away,
The powers of us may serve so great a day.

Come let us take a muster speedily,
Doomsday is near, die all, die merrily.
DOUGLAS: Talk not of dying, I am out of fear
Of death or death's hand for this one half year.

Exeunt.

IV. 2

Enter Falstaff and Bardolph.

FALSTAFF: Bardolph get thee before to Coventry, fill me
a bottle of sack, our soldiers shall march through. We 'll
to Sutton Cophill tonight.
BARDOLPH: Will you give me money captain?
FALSTAFF: Lay out, lay out.
BARDOLPH: This bottle makes an angel.
FALSTAFF: And if it do, take it for thy labour, and if it
make twenty take them all, I 'll answer the coinage.
Bid my Lieutenant Peto meet me at town's end.
BARDOLPH: I will captain, farewell.

Exit.

FALSTAFF: If I be not ashamed of my soldiers, I am a
sous'd gurnet; I have misused the king's press damn-
ably. I have got in exchange of a hundred and fifty
soldiers three hundred and odd pounds. I press me none
but good householders, Yeomen's sons, inquire me out
contracted bachelors, such as had been ask'd twice on
the banns, such a commodity of warm slaves, as had as
lieve hear the Devil as a drum, such as fear the report of
a caliver, worse than a struck fowl, or a hurt wild duck: I
press'd me none but such toasts and butter with hearts in
their bellies no bigger than pins' heads, and they have
bought out their services, and now my whole charge
consists of Ancients, Corporals, Lieutenants, gentlemen

of companies: slaves as ragged as Lazarus in the painted cloth, where the glutton's dogs licked his sores, and such as indeed were never soldiers, but discarded, unjust servingmen, younger sons to younger brothers, revolted tapsters, and ostlers, tradefallen, the cankers of a calm world, and a long peace, ten times more dishonourable ragged than an old fac'd ancient, and such have I to fill up the rooms of them as have bought out their services, that you would think that I had a hundred and fifty tottered prodigals, lately come from swine keeping, from eating draff and husks. A mad fellow met me on the way, and told me I had unloaded all the gibbets, and press'd the dead bodies. No eye hath seen such scarecrows. I'll not march through Coventry with them, that's flat: nay, and the villains march wide betwixt the legs as if they had gyves on, for indeed I had the most of them out of prison, there's but a shirt and a half in all my company, and the half shirt is two napkins tack'd together, and thrown over the shoulders like a Herald's coat without sleeves, and the shirt to say the truth stolen from my host at Saint Alban's, or the red-nose Innkeeper of Daventry, but that's all one, they'll find linen enough on every hedge.

Enter the Prince and the Lord of Westmoreland.

PRINCE: How now blown Jack? how now quilt?

FALSTAFF: What Hal, how now mad wag? what a devil dost thou in Warwickshire? My good Lord of Westmoreland, I cry you mercy, I thought your honour had already been at Shrewsbury.

WESTMORELAND: Faith Sir John 'tis more than time that I were there, and you too, but my powers are there already, the king I can tell you looks for us all, we must away all night.

D

FALSTAFF: Tut never fear me, I am as vigilant as a cat to steal cream.

PRINCE: I think to steal cream indeed, for thy theft hath already made thee butter, but tell me Jack, whose fellows are these that come after?

FALSTAFF: Mine Hal, mine.

PRINCE: I did never see such pitiful rascals.

FALSTAFF: Tut, tut, good enough to toss, food for powder, food for powder, they'll fill a pit as well as better; tush man, mortal men, mortal men.

WESTMORELAND: Ay but Sir John, methinks they are exceeding poor and bare, too beggarly.

FALSTAFF: Faith for their poverty I know not where they had that, and for their bareness I am sure they never learn'd that of me.

PRINCE: No I'll be sworn, unless you call three fingers in the ribs bare, but sirrah make haste, Percy is already in the field.

Exit.

FALSTAFF: What is the king encamp'd?

WESTMORELAND: He is Sir John, I fear we shall stay too long.

FALSTAFF: Well, to the latter end of a fray, and the beginning of a feast,

Fits a dull fighter and a keen guest.

Exeunt.

IV. 3

Enter Hotspur, Worcester, Douglas, Vernon.

HOTSPUR: We'll fight with him tonight.

WORCESTER: It may not be.

DOUGLAS: You give him then advantage.

VERNON: Not a whit.

HOTSPUR: Why say you so, looks he not for supply?

VERNON: So do we.

HOTSPUR: His is certain, ours is doubtful.

WORCESTER: Good cousin be advis'd, stir not tonight.

VERNON: Do not my Lord.

DOUGLAS: You do not counsel well,
    You speak it out of fear, and cold heart.

VERNON: Do me no slander Douglas, by my life,
    And I dare well maintain it with my life,
    If well respected honour bid me on,
    I hold as little counsel with weak fear,
    As you my Lord, or any Scot that this day lives,
    Let it be seen tomorrow in the battle which of us fears.

DOUGLAS: Yea or tonight.

VERNON: Content.

HOTSPUR: Tonight say I.

VERNON: Come, come, it may not be.
    I wonder much being men of such great leading as you
        are,
    That you foresee not what impediments
    Drag back our expedition, certain horse
    Of my cousin Vernon's are not yet come up.
    Your uncle Worcester's horse came but today,
    And now their pride and mettle is asleep,
    Their courage with hard labour tame and dull,
    That not a horse is half the half of himself.

HOTSPUR: So are the horses of the enemy
    In general journey bated and brought low,
    The better part of ours are full of rest.

WORCESTER: The number of the King exceedeth ours,
    For God's sake cousin stay till all come in.
        The trumpet sounds a parley. Enter Sir Walter Blunt.

BLUNT: I come with gracious offers from the king,
　　If you vouchsafe me hearing, and respect.
HOTSPUR: Welcome Sir Walter Blunt: and would to God
　　You were of our determination,
　　Some of us love you well, and even those some
　　Envy your great deservings and good name,
　　Because you are not of our quality,
　　But stand against us like an enemy.
BLUNT: And God defend but still I should stand so,
　　So long as out of limit and true rule
　　You stand against anointed Majesty.
　　But to my charge. The king hath sent to know
　　The nature of your griefs, and whereupon
　　You conjure from the breast of civil peace
　　Such bold hostility: teaching his duteous land
　　Audacious cruelty. If that the king
　　Have any way your good deserts forgot
　　Which he confesseth to be manifold,
　　He bids you name your griefs, and with all speed,
　　You shall have your desires with interest
　　And pardon absolute for yourself, and these
　　Herein misled by your suggestion.
HOTSPUR: The king is kind, and well we know the king
　　Knows at what time to promise, when to pay:
　　My father, and my uncle, and myself,
　　Did give him that same royalty he wears,
　　And when he was not six and twenty strong,
　　Sick in the world's regard: wretched and low,
　　A poor unminded outlaw sneaking home,
　　My father gave him welcome to the shore,
　　And when he heard him swear and vow to God,
　　He came but to be Duke of Lancaster,
　　To sue his livery, and beg his peace

With tears of innocency, and terms of zeal,
My father in kind heart and pity mov'd,
Swore him assistance, and perform'd it too.
Now when the Lords and Barons of the realm,
Perceiv'd Northumberland did lean to him,
The more and less came in with cap and knee,
Met him in Boroughs, Cities, Villages,
Attended him on bridges, stood in lanes,
Laid gifts before him, proffer'd him their oaths,
Gave him their heirs, as pages followed him,
Even at the heels, in golden multitudes.
He presently, as greatness knows itself,
Steps me a little higher than his vow
Made to my father while his blood was poor
Upon the naked shore at Ravenspurgh,
And now forsooth takes on him to reform
Some certain edicts, and some strait decrees,
That lie too heavy on the Common-wealth,
Cries out upon abuses, seems to weep
Over his Country's wrongs, and by this face
This seeming brow of justice did he win
The hearts of all that he did angle for:
Proceeded further, cut me off the heads
Of all the favourites that the absent king
In deputation left behind him here,
When he was personal in the Irish war.
BLUNT: Tut, I came not to hear this.
HOTSPUR: Then to the point.
In short time after he depos'd the king,
Soon after that depriv'd him of his life,
And in the neck of that task'd the whole state,
To make that worse, suffer'd his kinsman March
(Who is if every owner were well plac'd

Indeed his king) to be engag'd in Wales,
There without ransom to lie forfeited,
Disgrac'd me in my happy victories,
Sought to entrap me by intelligence,
Rated mine uncle from the council board,
In rage dismiss'd my father from the Court,
Broke oath on oath, committed wrong on wrong,
And in conclusion drove us to seek out
This head of safety, and withal to pry
Into his title, the which we find
Too indirect for long continuance.

BLUNT: Shall I return this answer to the King?

HOTSPUR: Not so Sir Walter. We'll withdraw a while.
Go to the king, and let there be impawn'd
Some surety for a safe return again,
And in the morning early shall mine uncle
Bring him our purposes, and so farewell.

BLUNT: I would you would accept of grace and love.

HOTSPUR: And may be so we shall.

BLUNT: Pray God you do.

Exeunt.

IV.4

Enter the Archbishop of York, Sir Michael.

ARCHBISHOP: Hie good Sir Michael, bear this sealed brief
With winged haste to the Lord Marshal,
This to my cousin Scroop, and all the rest
To whom they are directed. If you knew
How much they do import you would make haste.

SIR MICHAEL: My good Lord I guess their tenour.

ARCHBISHOP: Like enough you do.

Tomorrow good Sir Michael is a day,
Wherein the fortune of ten thousand men
Must bide the touch. For sir at Shrewsbury
As I am truly given to understand,
The king with mighty and quick-raised power
Meets with Lord Harry. And I fear Sir Michael
What with the sickness of Northumberland,
Whose power was in the first proportion,
And what with Owen Glendower's absence thence,
Who with them was a rated sinew too,
And comes not in overrul'd by prophecies,
I fear the power of Percy is too weak
To wage an instant trial with the king.

SIR MICHAEL: Why my good Lord, you need not fear,
There is Douglas, and Lord Mortimer.

ARCHBISHOP: No, Mortimer is not there.

SIR MICHAEL: But there is Mordake, Vernon, Lord Harry
Percy,
And there is my Lord of Worcester, and a head
Of gallant warriors, noble gentlemen.

ARCHBISHOP: And so there is: but yet the king hath
drawn
The special head of all the land together,
The Prince of Wales, Lord John of Lancaster,
The noble Westmoreland, and warlike Blunt,
And many mo corrivals and dear men
Of estimation and command in arms.

SIR MICHAEL: Doubt not my Lord: they shall be well
oppos'd

ARCHBISHOP: I hope no less; yet needful 'tis to fear,
And to prevent the worst, Sir Michael speed:
For if Lord Percy thrive not ere the king
Dismiss his power, he means to visit us,

For he hath heard of our confederacy,
And 'tis but wisdom to make strong against him,
Therefore make haste, I must go write again
To other friends, and so farewell Sir Michael.
                    Exeunt.

V. 1

Enter the King, the Prince of Wales, Lord John of Lancaster,
Earl of Westmoreland, Sir Walter Blunt, and Falstaff.

KING: How bloodily the sun begins to peer
    Above yon busky hill, the day looks pale
    At his distemp'rature.
PRINCE: The Southern wind
    Doth play the trumpet to his purposes,
    And by his hollow whistling in the leaves
    Foretells a tempest and a blust'ring day.
KING: Then with the losers let it sympathise,
    For nothing can seem foul to those that win.
                The trumpet sounds. Enter Worcester.
    How now my Lord of Worcester, 'tis not well,
    That you and I should meet upon such terms
    As now we meet. You have deceiv'd our trust,
    And made us doff our easy robes of peace,
    To crush our old limbs in ungentle steel,
    This is not well my Lord, this is not well.
    What say you to it? will you again unknit
    This churlish knot of all abhorred war?
    And move in that obedient orb again,
    Where you did give a fair, and natural light,
    And be no more an exhal'd meteor,
    A prodigy of fear, and a portent

Of broached mischief to the unborn times.

WORCESTER: Hear me my liege:
  For mine own part I could be well content,
  To entertain the lag-end of my life
  With quiet hours: For I do protest,
  I have not sought the day of this dislike.

KING: You have not sought it, how comes it then?

FALSTAFF: Rebellion lay in his way, and he found it.

PRINCE: Peace chewet, peace.

WORCESTER: It pleas'd your majesty to turn your looks
  Of favour from myself, and all our house,
  And yet I must remember you my Lord,
  We were the first and dearest of your friends,
  For you my staff of office did I break
  In Richard's time, and posted day and night
  To meet you on the way, and kiss your hand,
  When yet you were in place, and in account
  Nothing so strong and fortunate as I.
  It was myself, my brother and his son,
  That brought you home, and boldly did outdare
  The dangers of the time. You swore to us,
  And you did swear that oath at Doncaster,
  That you did nothing purpose 'gainst the state,
  Nor claim no further than your new fall'n right,
  The seat of Gaunt, Dukedom of Lancaster:
  To this we swore our aid: but in short space
  It rain'd down fortune show'ring on your head,
  And such a flood of greatness fell on you,
  What with our help, what with the absent king,
  What with the injuries of a wanton time,
  The seeming sufferances that you had borne,
  And the contrarious winds that held the king
  So long in his unlucky Irish wars,

That all in England did repute him dead:
And from this swarm of fair advantages,
You took occasion to be quickly wooed
To gripe the general sway into your hand,
Forgot your oath to us at Doncaster,
And being fed by us, you us'd us so
As that ungentle gull the cuckoo's bird
Useth the sparrow, did oppress our nest,
Grew by our feeding to so great a bulk,
That even our love durst not come near your sight,
For fear of swallowing: but with nimble wing
We were enforc'd for safety sake to fly
Out of your sight, and raise this present head,
Whereby we stand opposed by such means,
As you yourself have forg'd against yourself
By unkind usage, dangerous countenance,
And violation of all faith and troth,
Sworn to us in your younger enterprise.

KING: These things indeed you have articulate,
Proclaim'd at market Crosses, read in Churches,
To face the garment of rebellion
With some fine colour that may please the eye
Of fickle changelings and poor discontents,
Which gape and rub the elbow at the news
Of hurly burly innovation,
And never yet did insurrection want
Such watercolours to impaint his cause
Nor moody beggars starving for a time,
Of pell mell havoc and confusion.

PRINCE: In both your armies there is many a soul,
Shall pay full dearly for this encounter,
If once they join in trial, tell your nephew
The Prince of Wales doth join with all the world

In praise of Henry Percy, by my hopes
This present enterprise set off his head,
I do not think a braver Gentleman,
More active, valiant, or more valiant young,
More daring, or more bold is now alive
To grace this latter age with noble deeds.
For my part I may speak it to my shame,
I have a truant been to Chivalry,
And so I hear he doth account me too;
Yet this before my father's majesty,
I am content that he shall take the odds
Of his great name and estimation,
And will to save the blood on either side
Try fortune with him in a single fight.

KING: And Prince of Wales, so dare we venture thee,
Albeit, considerations infinite
Do make against it: no good Worcester no,
We love our people well, even those we love
That are misled upon your cousin's part,
And will they take the offer of our grace,
Both he, and they, and you, yea every man
Shall be my friend again, and I 'll be his,
So tell your cousin, and bring me word
What he will do. But if he will not yield,
Rebuke and dread correction wait on us,
And they shall do their office. So be gone:
We will not now be troubled with reply,
We offer fair, take it advisedly.

Exit Worcester.

PRINCE: It will not be accepted on my life,
The Douglas and the Hotspur both together,
Are confident against the world in arms.

KING: Hence therefore, every leader to his charge,

For on their answer will we set on them,
And God befriend us as our cause is just.

Exeunt: manent Prince and Falstaff.

FALSTAFF: Hal, if thou see me down in the battle and bestride me, so, 'tis a point of friendship.

PRINCE: Nothing but a Colossus can do thee that friendship, say thy prayers, and farewell.

FALSTAFF: I would 'twere bed time Hal, and all well.

PRINCE: Why, thou owest God a death.

Exit.

FALSTAFF: 'Tis not due yet, I would be loath to pay him before his day, what need I be so forward with him that calls not on me? Well, 'tis no matter, honour pricks me on; yea, but how if honour prick me off when I come on? how then? can honour set to a leg? no, or an arm? no, or take away the grief of a wound? no, honour hath no skill in surgery then? no, what is honour? a word, what is in that word honour? what is that honour? air, a trim reckoning. Who hath it? he that died a' Wednesday, doth he feel it? no, doth he hear it? no, 'tis insensible then? yea, to the dead, but will it not live with the living? no, why? detraction will not suffer it, therefore I 'll none of it, honour is a mere scutcheon, and so ends my Catechism.

Exit.

V. 2

Enter Worcester, Sir Richard Vernon.

WORCESTER: O no, my nephew must not know Sir Richard,
The liberal and kind offer of the king.

VERNON: 'Twere best he did.
WORCESTER: Then are we all undone.
  It is not possible, it cannot be
  The king should keep his word in loving us,
  He will suspect us still, and find a time
  To punish this offence in other faults,
  Suspicion all our lives shall be stuck full of eyes,
  For treason is but trusted like the Fox,
Who never so tame, so cherish'd and lock'd up,
  Will have a wild trick of his ancestors,
  Look how we can, or sad or merrily,
  Interpretation will misquote our looks,
  And we shall feed like oxen at a stall,
  The better cherish'd still the nearer death.
  My nephew's trespass may be well forgot,
  It hath the excuse of youth and heat of blood,
  And an adopted name of privilege,
  A hare-brain'd Hotspur govern'd by a spleen,
  All his offences live upon my head
  And on his father's. We did train him on,
  And his corruption being ta'en from us,
  We as the spring of all shall pay for all:
  Therefore good cousin, let not Harry know
  In any case the offer of the King.
            Enter Hotspur and Douglas.
VERNON: Deliver what you will, I 'll say tis so.
  Here comes your cousin.
HOTSPUR: My uncle is return'd,
  Deliver up my Lord of Westmoreland.
  Uncle, what news?
WORCESTER: The king will bid you battle presently.
DOUGLAS: Defy him by the Lord of Westmoreland.
HOTSPUR: Lord Douglas go you and tell him so.

DOUGLAS: Marry and shall, and very willingly.
Exit Douglas.
WORCESTER: There is no seeming mercy in the king.
HOTSPUR: Did you beg any? God forbid.
WORCESTER: I told him gently of our grievances,
Of his oath breaking, which he mended thus,
By now forswearing that he is forsworn,
He calls us rebels, traitors, and will scourge
With haughty arms this hateful name in us.
Enter Douglas.
DOUGLAS: Arm gentlemen, to arms, for I have thrown
A brave defiance in King Henry's teeth,
And Westmoreland that was engag'd did bear it,
Which cannot choose but bring him quickly on.
WORCESTER: The Prince of Wales stepp'd forth before
the King,
And nephew, challeng'd you to single fight.
HOTSPUR: O would the quarrel lay upon our heads,
And that no man might draw short breath today
But I and Harry Monmouth; tell me, tell me,
How show'd his tasking? seem'd it in contempt?
VERNON: No, by my soul I never in my life
Did hear a challenge urg'd more modestly,
Unless a brother should a brother dare,
To gentle exercise and proof of arms.
He gave you all the duties of a man,
Trimm'd up your praises with a princely tongue,
Spoke your deservings like a Chronicle,
Making you ever better than his praise,
By still dispraising praise valued with you,
And which became him like a prince indeed,
He made a blushing cital of himself,
And chid his truant youth with such a grace

As if he master'd there a double spirit
Of teaching and of learning instantly,
There did he pause, but let me tell the world
If he outlive the envy of this day,
England did never owe so sweet a hope
So much misconstrued in his wantonness.

HOTSPUR: Cousin I think thou art enamoured
On his follies, never did I hear
Of any prince so wild a liberty,
But be he as he will, yet once ere night
I will embrace him with a soldier's arm,
That he shall shrink under my courtesy.
Arm, arm with speed, and fellows, soldiers, friends,
Better consider what you have to do
Than I that have not well the gift of tongue
Can lift your blood up with persuasion.

Enter a Messenger.

MESSENGER: My Lord, here are letters for you.

HOTSPUR: I cannot read them now.
O Gentlemen the time of life is short,
To spend that shortness basely were too long
If life did ride upon a dial's point,
Still ending at the arrival of an hour,
And if we live we live to tread on kings,
If die, brave death when princes die with us,
Now for our consciences, the arms are fair
When the intent of bearing them is just.

Enter another Messenger.

MESSENGER: My Lord prepare, the king comes on apace.

HOTSPUR: I thank him that he cuts me from my tale,
For I profess not talking, only this,
Let each man do his best, and here draw I
A sword, whose temper I intend to stain

With the best blood that I can meet withal,
In the adventure of this perilous day.
Now esperance Percy, and set on:
Sound all the lofty instruments of war,
And by that music let us all embrace,
For heaven to earth some of us never shall
A second time do such a courtesy.

Here they embrace and exeunt. The trumpets sound.
The King enters with his power; alarm to the battle.
Exeunt. Then enter Douglas, and Sir Walter Blunt.

V. 3

BLUNT: What is thy name that in the battle thus thou
crossest me,
What honour dost thou seek upon my head?
DOUGLAS: Know then my name is Douglas,
And I do haunt thee in the battle thus
Because some tell me that thou art a king.
BLUNT: They tell thee true.
DOUGLAS: The Lord of Stafford dear today hath bought
Thy likeness, for instead of thee King Harry
This sword hath ended him, so shall it thee
Unless thou yield thee as my prisoner.
BLUNT: I was not born a yielder thou proud Scot,
And thou shall find a king that will revenge
Lord Stafford's death.

They fight. Douglas kills Blunt. Then enter Hotspur.

HOTSPUR: O Douglas hadst thou fought at Holmedon thus
I never had triumph'd upon a Scot.
DOUGLAS: All 's done, all 's won, here breathless lies the
king.
HOTSPUR: Where?

DOUGLAS: Here.

HOTSPUR: This Douglas? no, I know this face full well,
A gallant knight he was, his name was Blunt,
Semblably furnish'd like the king himself.

DOUGLAS: Ah fool, go with thy soul whither it goes,
A borrowed title hast thou bought too dear.
Why didst thou tell me that thou wert a king?

HOTSPUR: The king hath many marching in his coats.

DOUGLAS: Now by my sword I will kill all his coats,
I 'll murder all his wardrobe, piece by piece
Until I meet the king.

HOTSPUR: Up and away,
Our soldiers stand full fairly for the day.

Exeunt.

Alarum. Enter Falstaff solus.

FALSTAFF: Though I could 'scape shot-free at London,
I fear the shot here, here 's no scoring but upon the
pate. Soft, who are you? Sir Walter Blunt, there 's
honour for you, here 's no vanity, I am as hot as molten
lead, and as heavy too: God keep lead out of me, I
need no more weight than mine own bowels. I have led
my ragamuffins where they are pepper'd, there 's not
three of my hundred and fifty left alive, and they are for
the town's end, to beg during life: but who comes here?

Enter the Prince.

PRINCE: What, stand'st thou idle here? lend me thy
sword,
Many a nobleman lies stark and stiff,
Under the hoofs of vaunting enemies,
Whose deaths are yet unreveng'd, I prithee lend me thy
sword.

FALSTAFF: O Hal, I prithee give me leave to breathe a
while, Turk Gregory never did such deeds in arms as I

have done this day, I have paid Percy, I have made him sure.

PRINCE: He is indeed, and living to kill thee:
I prithee lend me thy sword.

FALSTAFF: Nay before God Hal, if Percy be alive thou gets not my sword, but take my pistol if thou wilt.

PRINCE: Give it me, what? is it in the case?

FALSTAFF: Ay Hal, 'tis hot, 'tis hot, there 's that will sack a city.

The Prince draws it out, and finds it to be a bottle of sack.

PRINCE: What is it a time to jest and dally now?

He throws the bottle at him. Exit.

FALSTAFF: Well if Percy be alive, I 'll pierce him; if he do come in my way so, if he do not, if I come in his willingly, let him make a carbonado of me. I like not such grinning honour as Sir Walter hath, give me life, which if I can save, so: if not, honour comes unlook'd for, and there 's an end.

Exit.

V.4

Alarum. Excursions. Enter the King, the Prince, Lord John of Lancaster, and Earl of Westmoreland.

KING: I prithee Harry withdraw thyself, thou bleedest too much,
Lord John of Lancaster go you with him.

LANCASTER: Not I my Lord, unless I did bleed too.

PRINCE: I beseech your majesty make up,
Lest your retirement do amaze your friends.

KING: I will do so. My Lord of Westmoreland lead him to his tent.

WESTMORELAND: Come my Lord, I 'll lead you to your
tent.
PRINCE: Lead me my Lord? I do not need your help,
And God forbid a shallow scratch should drive
The Prince of Wales from such a field as this,
Where stain'd nobility lies trodden on,
And rebels' arms triumph in massacres.
LANCASTER: We breathe too long, come cousin West-
moreland
Our duty this way lies: For God's sake come.
Exeunt Prince John and Westmoreland.
PRINCE: By God thou hast deceiv'd me Lancaster,
I did not think thee Lord of such a spirit,
Before I lov'd thee as a brother John,
But now I do respect thee as my soul.
KING: I saw him hold Lord Percy at the point,
With lustier maintenance than I did look for
Of such an ungrown warrior.
PRINCE: O this boy lends mettle to us all.
Exit.
Enter Douglas.
DOUGLAS: Another king, they grow like Hydra's heads
I am the Douglas fatal to all those
That wear those colours on them. What art thou
That counterfeit'st the person of a King?
KING HENRY: The king himself, who Douglas grieves at
heart,
So many of his shadows thou hast met
And not the very king, I have two boys
Seek Percy and thyself about the field,
But seeing thou fall'st on me so luckily
I will assay thee and defend thyself.
DOUGLAS: I fear thou art another counterfeit,

And yet in faith thou bearest thee like a king,
But mine I am sure thou art whoe'er thou be,
And thus I win thee.
> *They fight, the King being in danger, enter Prince of Wales.*

PRINCE: Hold up thy head vile Scot, or thou art like
Never to hold it up again, the spirits
Of valiant Shirley, Stafford, Blunt are in my arms,
It is the Prince of Wales that threatens thee,
Who never promiseth but he means to pay.
> *They fight. Douglas flieth.*

Cheerly my Lord, how fares your grace?
Sir Nicholas Gawsey hath for succour sent,
And so hath Clifton, I 'll to Clifton straight.
KING: Stay and breathe awhile,
Thou hast redeem'd thy lost opinion,
And show'd thou mak'st some tender of my life,
In this fair rescue thou hast brought to me.
PRINCE: O God they did me too much injury,
That ever said I hearken'd for your death,
If it were so, I might have let alone
The insulting hand of Douglas over you,
Which would have been as speedy in your end
As all the poisonous potions in the world,
And sav'd the treacherous labour of your son.
KING: Make up to Clifton, I 'll to Sir Nicholas Gawsey.
> *Exit King.*
> *Enter Hotspur.*

HOTSPUR: If I mistake not, thou art Harry Monmouth.
PRINCE: Thou speak'st as if I would deny my name.
HOTSPUR: My name is Harry Percy.
PRINCE: Why then I see a very valiant rebel of the name;
I am the Prince of Wales, and think not Percy

To share with me in glory any more:
Two stars keep not their motion in one sphere,
Nor can one England brook a double reign
Of Harry Percy and the Prince of Wales.

HOTSPUR: Nor shall it Harry, for the hour is come
To end the one of us, and would to God
Thy name in arms were now as great as mine.

PRINCE: I 'll make it greater ere I part from thee,
And all the budding honours on thy crest
I 'll crop to make a garland for my head.

HOTSPUR: I can no longer brook thy vanities.

They fight. Enter Falstaff.

FALSTAFF: Well said Hal, to it Hal. Nay you shall find
no boy's play here I can tell you.

*Enter Douglas, he fighteth with Falstaff; he falls down
as if he were dead, and exit Douglas. The Prince
killeth Percy.*

HOTSPUR: Oh Harry thou hast robb'd me of my youth,
I better brook the loss of brittle life
Than those proud titles thou hast won of me,
They wound my thoughts worse than thy sword my
flesh,
But thought 's the slave of life, and life time's fool,
And time that takes survey of all the world
Must have a stop. O I could prophesy,
But that the earthy and cold hand of death
Lies on my tongue: no Percy thou art dust
And food for —

PRINCE: For worms, brave Percy. Fare thee well great
heart:
Ill weav'd ambition, how much art thou shrunk?
When that this body did contain a spirit,
A kingdom for it was too small a bound,

But now two paces of the vilest earth
Is room enough, this earth that bears thee dead
Bears not alive so stout a gentleman.
If thou wert sensible of courtesy
I should not make so dear a show of zeal,
But let my favours hide thy mangled face,
And even in thy behalf I 'll thank myself,
For doing these fair rites of tenderness.
Adieu and take thy praise with thee to heaven,
Thy ignominy sleep with thee in the grave,
But not remember'd in thy epitaph.

He spieth Falstaff on the ground.

What old acquaintance, could not all this flesh
Keep in a little life? poor Jack farewell,
I could have better spar'd a better man:
O I should have a heavy miss of thee,
If I were much in love with vanity:
Death hath not struck so fat a Deer today,
Though many dearer in this bloody fray,
Embowell'd will I see thee by and by,
Till then in blood by noble Percy lie.

Exit.

Falstaff riseth up.

FALSTAFF: Embowell'd, if thou embowel me today, I 'll
give you leave to powder me and eat me too tomorrow.
'Zblood 'twas time to counterfeit, or that hot termagant
Scot had paid me scot and lot too. Counterfeit? I lie, I
am no counterfeit, to die is to be a counterfeit, for he is
but the counterfeit of a man, who hath not the life of a
man: but to counterfeit dying when a man thereby
liveth, is to be no counterfeit, but the true and perfect
image of life indeed. The better part of valour is dis-
cretion, in the which better part I have saved my life.

'Zounds I am afraid of this gunpowder Percy, though he be dead, how if he should counterfeit too and rise? by my faith I am afraid he would prove the better counterfeit, therefore I 'll make him sure, yea, and I 'll swear I kill'd him. Why may not he rise as well as I? nothing confutes me but eyes, and nobody sees me: therefore sirrah, with a new wound in your thigh, come you along with me.

Takes up Hotspur on his back. Enter the Prince of
Wales and Lord John of Lancaster.

PRINCE: Come brother John, full bravely hast thou flesh'd
Thy maiden sword.
LANCASTER: But soft, whom have we here?
Did you not tell me this fat man was dead?
PRINCE: I did, I saw him dead,
Breathless and bleeding on the ground. Art thou alive?
Or is it fantasy that plays upon our eyesight?
I prithee speak, we will not trust our eyes
Without our ears, thou art not what thou seem'st.
FALSTAFF: No that's certain, I am not a double man: but if I be not Jack Falstaff, then am I a Jack: there is Percy, if your father will do me any honour, so: if not, let him kill the next Percy himself: I look to be either Earl or Duke, I can assure you.
PRINCE: Why Percy, I kill'd myself, and saw thee dead.
FALSTAFF: Didst thou? Lord, Lord, how this world is given to lying, I grant you I was down, and out of breath, and so was he, but we rose both at an instant, and fought a long hour by Shrewsbury clock: if I may be believ'd, so; if not, let them that should reward valour, bear the sin upon their own heads, I 'll take it upon my death, I gave him this wound in the thigh, if

the man were alive, and would deny it, 'zounds I would
make him eat a piece of my sword.

LANCASTER: This is the strangest tale that ever I heard.

PRINCE: This is the strangest fellow, brother John:
Come bring your luggage nobly on your back.
For my part, if a lie may do thee grace,
I 'll gild it with the happiest terms I have.

A retreat is sounded.

The trumpet sounds retreat, the day is ours,
Come brother let us to the highest of the field,
To see what friends are living, who are dead.

Exeunt Prince of Wales and Lancaster.

FALSTAFF: I 'll follow as they say for reward. He that
rewards me God reward him. If I do grow great, I 'll
grow less, for I 'll purge and leave sack, and live cleanly
as a noble man should do.

Exit.

V. 5

The trumpets sound. Enter the King, Prince of Wales,
Lord John of Lancaster, Earl of Westmoreland, with Worcester
and Vernon prisoners.

KING: Thus ever did rebellion find rebuke.
Ill spirited Worcester, did not we send grace,
Pardon, and terms of love to all of you?
And wouldst thou turn our offers contrary?
Misuse the tenour of thy kinsman's trust?
Three knights upon our party slain today,
A noble Earl and many a creature else,
Had been alive this hour,
If like a Christian thou hadst truly borne

Betwixt our armies true intelligence.

WORCESTER: What I have done my safety urg'd me to:
  And I embrace this fortune patiently,
  Since not to be avoided it falls on me.

KING: Bear Worcester to the death and Vernon too:
  Other offenders we will pause upon.

  Exeunt Worcester and Vernon.

  How goes the field?

PRINCE: The noble Scot Lord Douglas, when he saw
  The fortune of the day quite turn'd from him,
  The noble Percy slain and all his men
  Upon the foot of fear, fled with the rest
  And falling from a hill, he was so bruis'd,
  That the pursuers took him. At my tent
  The Douglas is: and I beseech your grace
  I may dispose of him.

KING: With all my heart.

PRINCE: Then brother John of Lancaster,
  To you this honourable bounty shall belong,
  Go to the Douglas and deliver him
  Up to his pleasure, ransomless and free,
  His valour shown upon our crests today
  Hath taught us how to cherish such high deeds,
  Even in the bosom of our adversaries.

LANCASTER: I thank your grace for this high courtesy,
  Which I shall give away immediately.

KING: Then this remains that we divide our power.
  You son John, and my cousin Westmoreland
  Towards York shall bend you, with your dearest speed
  To meet Northumberland and the Prelate Scroop,
  Who as we hear are busily in arms:
  Myself and you son Harry will towards Wales,
  To fight with Glendower and the Earl of March.

Rebellion in this land shall lose his sway,
Meeting the check of such another day,
And since this business so fair is done,
Let us not leave till all our own be won.

Exeunt.

.NOTES

References are to the page and line of this edition; there are 33 lines to a full page.

The Actors' Names. Edmund Mortimer, Earl of March: P. 22 L. 10
The relationship between Henry IV and the Mortimers is complicated. Edward III had six sons, of whom the eldest was Edward the Black Prince, the second was Lionel Duke of Clarence, and the third John of Gaunt Duke of Lancaster. Edward III outlived the Black Prince. When Edward III died he was succeeded by his grandson, the Black Prince's son, Richard II. As Richard II died without children, the next in order of legal succession was the senior descendant of Lionel. Lionel left no male heirs; but his daughter Philippa had married Edmund Earl of March. They had three children – Roger (who became Earl of March and died in 1398), Elizabeth (who married Hotspur and is thus the 'Lady Percy' of *I Henry IV*) and Edmund who was captured by Glendower and married Glendower's daughter (all three appear in III. 1 of the play). This Edmund, though referred to as 'Earl of March' was not in fact Earl of March. The real Edmund (II) Earl of March was the eldest son of *Roger Mortimer*. Shakespeare has thus confused the two Edmunds; the husband of Glendower's daughter had no claim on the English throne. Henry IV himself was eldest son and heir of John of Gaunt, third son of Edward III.

Bardolph: in the 1st Quarto his name is given as Bardoll.
P. 22 L. 20

Find we: let us find.
P. 23 L. 5

short winded: breathless talk.
P. 23 L. 6

thirsty entrance: i.e. the dry earth sopping up the blood.
P. 23 L. 8

meteors . . . heaven: eyes flashing like meteors which herald disaster.
P. 23 L. 13

P. 23 L. 16   *close:* hand to hand combat.

P. 24 L. 6   *dear expedience:* urgent enterprise, dear to my heart.

P. 24 L. 7   *hot in question:* eagerly debated.

P. 24 L. 9   *limits of the charge:* estimates of the cost.

P. 24 L. 10   *all athwart:* cutting across the debate.

P. 24 L. 27   *Holy rood day:* September 14.

P. 24 L. 28   *Young Harry Percy:* Shakespeare depicts Hotspur as a rash youth of about the same age as Prince Hal. Actually at the battle of Shrewsbury (1403), Hal was barely 14 years old, and Hotspur was 39.

P. 24 LL. 32–3   *by discharge . . . was told:* i.e. the sound of the artillery indicated a fierce battle.

P. 26 LL. 1–3   *The prisoners . . . he keeps:* There was a similar incident at Court in the autumn of 1596, when the Earl of Essex refused to surrender the ransoms of the Spanish prisoners taken at Cadiz to Queen Elizabeth. When Lord Burghley suggested the Queen should first consider the terms on which they surrendered she turned on him as a miscreant and a coward who either for fear or favour regarded Essex more than herself.

P. 26 L. 7   *Malevolent . . . aspects:* like an ill-omened planet universally disastrous.

P. 26 L. 17   *out of anger:* from an angry heart.

P. 26 L. 24   *sack:* a dry Spanish wine to which Sir John was very partial.

P. 27 L. 4   *go by:* tell the time by – as later (P. 43 L 3) the carrier tells the time by Charles' Wain.

P. 27 L. 11   *egg and butter:* fasting fare, for which a very brief grace sufficed.

P. 27 L. 14   *squires of the nights' body:* gentlemen of the dark (i.e highwaymen).

P. 27 L. 15   *thieves . . . day's beauty:* i.e. loafers, are a pun on *beauty* and *booty.*

P. 27 L. 15   *Diana's foresters:* Diana was Goddess of Hunting, and also of the Moon. Her foresters therefore hunt by moonlight.

good government : respectable life. P. 27 L. 16

lay by : i.e. 'stand and deliver', 'stick 'em up'. *bring* P. 27 L. 25
in : i.e. the drink. and L. 26

ladder : from which the condemned was 'turned off' P. 27 L. 27
the gallows.

old lad of the castle : a tough. Shakespeare probably P. 27 L. 31
used the phrase as a pun on Falstaff's first incarnation
as Oldcastle. (See p. 18.)

buff jerkin : the sergeant's leather coat – not a wel- P. 27 L. 32
come sight to thieves. *robe of durance :* a coat that
wears well and also that takes you to durance (i.e.,
jail).

quips . . . quiddities : sharp witty sayings and quibbles. P. 28 L. 1

suits . . . hangman . . . wardrobe : The clothes of P. 28
the executed were the hangman's valuable perquisite. LL. 26–7
This sometimes led to unseemly wrangle. When
George Brooke was executed on 8th December 1603,
for his share in the Main and Bye Plot, he appeared
on the scaffold wearing a black damask gown, which
was handed to the Sheriff's men. The headsman
demanded it and refused to move until he had it.

gib cat : a castrated cat. The phrase still exists in P. 28 L. 28
Ireland – 'as cross as a cut cat'.

melancholy of Moorditch : Evil smells were supposed P. 28
to be a cause of melancholy, and Moorditch was LL. 32–3
renowned for its stench. 'This Ditch being originally
made for the defence of the City, was also long
together, carefully cleansed and maintained as need
required, but now of late neglected and forced
either to a very narrow and the same a filthy channel,
or altogether stopped up for gardens planted and
houses builded thereon, even to the very wall, and
in many places upon both ditch and wall houses
to be builded, to what danger of the City, I leave to
wiser consideration : and can but wish that reformation might be had.' [Stow's *Survey of London,* ed.
C. L. Kingsford, i. 19.]

comparative : full of witty similes. P. 29 L. 1

P. 29 L. 9   *wisdom cries out . . . :* a free quotation from *Proverbs* i: 20–24.

P. 29 L. 11   *damnable iteration:* a wicked habit of quotation.

P. 29 L. 15   *one of the wicked:* Falstaff here, and later at L. 24 – ''tis no sin for a man to labour in his vocation', – mimics the Puritan fashion of talking in a Scriptural jargon.

P. 29 L. 21   *baffle:* disgrace. The word is used of the disgracing of a knight found guilty of breaking his oath. He was stripped of his armour, his shield painted with the coat of arms reversed, and his picture or effigy hung upside down.

P. 29 L. 27   *set a match:* planned a hold-up.

P. 29 L. 33   *Sack, and Sugar:* Englishmen liked their wine sweet.

P. 30   *Good Friday . . . capon's leg:* To eat meat on Good
LL. 2–3   Friday, the Church's most solemn fast day, was damnable.

P. 30 L. 19   *Yedward:* a familiar form of Edward, Poins' Christian name.

P. 30 L. 26   *royal . . . ten shillings:* one of several common puns on the names and values of coins. A 'royal' and an 'angel' were worth 10s.

P. 31 L. 3   *God give thee . . . :* more Puritanical talk.

P. 31 L. 7   *want countenance:* need someone to give them an air of respectability.

P. 31 L. 9   *All-hallown summer:* the patch of fine weather sometimes experienced in an English autumn, called also an Indian summer, and applied to a man who is hale in his old age. All-Hallows Day is 1st November.

P. 31 L. 14   *Bardolph, Peto:* In the Quarto, 'Harvey, Rossill'.

P. 31 L. 30   *cases of buckram:* coarse linen overalls.

P. 32   *uphold . . . idleness:* put up with your unrestrained,
LL. 13–14   idle behaviour.

P. 32 L. 16   *contagious clouds:* clouds and fogs were believed to bring sickness.

P. 32 L. 33   *foil:* a thin leaf of bright metal placed behind a precious stone to make it sparkle.

Redeeming time: making up for lost time.   P. 33 L. 2

found me: found me out.   P. 33 L. 9

moody ... brow: the frowning forehead of a dis- P. 33 L. 25
gruntled subject.

chin new reaped: his beard clipped close.   P. 34 L. 11

pouncet-box: a small box of perfume, used by the P. 34 L. 15
fastidious to counteract the many noisome stenches.

Took it in snuff: (*lit.*) snuffed it up, and (*proverbially*) P. 34 L. 18
was indignant, or 'snuffy'.

God save the mark: an impatient apology for a coarse P. 34 L. 33
remark.

parmaceti: spermaceti, a fatty substance found in the P. 35 L. 2
whale and much esteemed as an ointment.

bald unjointed: slight disconnected.   P. 35 L. 9

Come current: be regarded as valid.   P. 35 L. 12

Earl of March: see note on P. 22, L. 10   P. 35 L. 28

indent with: make an agreement with.   P. 35 L. 31

changing hardiment: exchanging blows.   P. 36 L. 12

Colour her working: disguise its sinister intention.   P. 36 L. 20

sirrah: a term of address used to an inferior, here P. 36 L. 28
deliberately insulting.

ingrate and canker'd: ungrateful and corrupted P. 37 L. 18
(literally 'maggoty').

blot ... subornation: disgrace of being a murderer's P. 38
accomplice.   LL. 13–14

unsteadfast ... spear: i.e., with only a spear as bridge. P. 39 L. 12

apprehends ... figures: i.e., he is entirely carried away P. 39 L. 28
by his imagination.

sword and buckler: swash-buckler.   P. 40 L. 19

politician: frequently used in a sinister and con- P. 40 L. 32
temptuous way.

At Berkley-castle: for this episode, see *Richard II*, P. 41 L. 7
III. 3.

candy deal of courtesy: a deal of sugary compliment. P. 41 L. 9

in estimation: at a guess.   P. 41 L. 31

let'st slip: release the greyhound too soon.   P. 42 L. 5

P. 42 L. 12   *raising of a head:* raising a rebellious army.

P. 43 L. 4   *Charles' wain:* the constellation of the Great Bear.

P. 43 L. 8   *flocks in the point:* loose wool in the pommel.

P. 43 L. 9   *out of all cess:* excessively.

P. 43 L. 17   *tench:* certain fish, especially the tench and loach, harbour a kind of louse.

P. 43 L. 22   *chamber-lie:* urine. Elizabethan sanitary arrangements and domestic habits were crude.

P. 44 L. 11   *Ay when canst tell?:* 'sez you'.

P. 44 L. 20   *Enter Chamberlain:* The chamberlain was in charge of the bedrooms in an inn. Chamberlains were reputed to be in league with highwaymen to whom they reported the movements of guests.

P. 45 L. 13   *foot landrakers:* footpads – too poor to have horses.

P. 45 LL. 13–14   *long-staff sixpenny strikers:* thieves who will knock a man down for sixpence with their long staffs.

P. 45 LL. 14–15   *mad ... malt-worms:* red-faced tipplers with great mustaches.

P. 45 L. 16   *Oneyers:* spelt 'oneyres' in the Quarto: perhaps a slang word for great ones.

P. 45 L. 26   *fern-seed:* the seed of certain fern is so small as to be imperceptible. If found it was believed to confer invisibility on the finder.

P. 46 L. 8   *frets ... gumm'd velvet:* Inferior velvet (treated with gum to make it appear of good quality) which soon fretted.

P. 47 L. 21   *ballads:* Any notable scandal was quickly celebrated in doggerel songs made by ballad-mongers.

P. 47 L. 27   *setter:* in thieves' language the confederate who first brings in the victim.

P. 48 L. 19   *happy man be his dole:* good luck to all.

P. 49 L. 2   *grand jurors:* the grand jury was composed of wealthy and respectable citizens.

P. 51 L. 9   *treasures ... of thee:* my right to enjoy your valued company.

P. 51 L. 17   *Of basilisks, of cannon, culverin:* various types of Elizabethan cannon. The *basilisk* was of 5-inch calibre and fired a shot of 15½ lb. The *cannon* of 8-inch calibre fired a 60 lb. shot. The *culverin* was of 5½ inch calibre and fired a 17 lb. shot.

Esperance : the battle-cry of the Percy family.   P. 52 L. 5

base-string of humility : i.e., sunk to the lowest depth.   P. 53 L. 28

leash of drawers : a set of three.   P. 53 LL. 28–9

Corinthian : (like Trojan) a good fellow.   P. 54 L. 2

a good boy : To be called 'boy' by one of his own P. 54 L. 3 standing would have been an insult; but the drawers have their own pothouse vocabulary.

cry hem : a drinking cry, like 'cheerio'.   P. 54 L. 6

play it off : toss it down.   P. 54 L. 7

anon, anon sir : 'coming sir.'   P. 54 L. 16

Half-moon : the rooms of an inn each had names.   P. 54 L. 17

present : an example. Some editors alter to 'pre- P. 54 L. 22 cedent'.

Pomgarnet : Pomegranate, another of the rooms.   P. 54 LL. 28–9

indenture : agreement to serve as apprentice.   P. 55 L. 5

leathern jerkin ... Spanish pouch : This list gives the P. 55 outward characteristics of a prosperous innkeeper— LL. 26–8 leather coat with crystal buttons, cropped head (*not-pated*), large ring, grey (*puke*) stockings, worsted (*caddis*) garters, and a pouch of Spanish leather.

Why ... much : The Prince is deliberately speaking P. 55 nonsense to complete the befuddlement of Francis.   LL. 30–2

parcel of a reckoning : the details of the bill.   P. 56 LL. 27–8

Rivo : another drinking cry.   P. 57 L. 3

sew netherstocks : make stockings – a humble, P. 57 L. 9 sweated occupation.

pitiful hearted Titan ... of the sun's : a difficult P. 57 and probably corrupted sentence: Titan is the sun, LL. 14–15 and so does not melt. The best emendation is to omit Titan which may have been accidentally repeated by the printer.

lime : lime was used to adulterate wine to give it P. 57 L. 16 a better taste and colour.

E

P. 57 L. 22	*shotten herring:* a herring that has discharged its roe.
P. 57 L. 25	*weaver:* Most of the weavers were Protestant refugees from Flanders, noted for their psalm-singing.
P. 57 L. 29	*dagger of lath:* wooden dagger.
P. 58 L. 23	*at half-sword:* at close-quarters – the cautious fighter kept at a greater distance.
P. 58 L. 27	*ecce signum:* behold the sign.
P. 59 L. 20	*ward:* position of defence. Here Falstaff re-enacts his version of his heroic action.
P. 59 L. 27	*took ... points in my target:* the buckler (or target) was a small light shield intended to catch and break the opponent's point.
P. 60 L. 5	*points being broken:* a pun on *points:* laces to fasten the hose to the doublet.
P. 60 L. 13	*Kendal green:* so called because the cloth was made at Kendal in Westmorland.
P. 60 L. 19	*tallow-catch:* variously emended to *tallow-ketch:* a tub for tallow, or *tallow-keech:* a lump of tallow: but *tallow-catch* would naturally mean 'a thing for catching tallow', i.e., the rim round the lip of a candle-stick, which piled up with the candle-drippings is no bad simile for Falstaff.
P. 60 L. 28	*strappado:* a torture. The victim's hands were tied behind his back: he was then hoisted by the arms to a considerable height and let drop.
P. 61 L. 3	*elfskin:* In Shakespeare's company there was a tall thin actor whose proportions are often mocked. *Elf-skin* is sometimes emended to 'eel-skin'. The Bastard in *King John* talks of his brother's arms as 'eel-skins stripped'. If *elf-skin* is right it probably means 'a sloughed snake-skin'. As Oberon puts it: And there the snake throws her enamelled skin, Weed wide enough to wrap a fairy in.
P. 61 L. 6	*standing tuck:* rapier stuck in the ground.
P.61 LL.28-9	*lion ... prince:* This was very generally believed.
P. 62 LL. 11-15	*noble-man ... royal man:* another pun on money; a *noble:* 6s. 8d.; a *royal:* 10s.

taken . . . manner: caught in the act.   P. 63 L. 6

meteors . . . exhalations: Bardolph indicates his own   P. 63
fiery face which (he claims) is proof that he is a man   LL. 10–11
of wrath; *exhalation:* meteor.

Choler . . . halter: choler (anger) and *collar* were   P. 63
pronounced alike, hence a never failing pun.   LL. 15–17

O Glendower: Probably Shakespeare's abbreviation   P. 63 L. 32
of Owen, which the printer had mistaken for 'O'.

state: chair of state, royal throne.   P. 65 L. 3

King Cambyses' vein: Cambyses is the hero of   P. 65 L. 12
'A Lamentable Tragedy, mixed full of pleasant
mirth', published in 1570, and one of the earliest
surviving plays performed on a public stage. It is
written in a ranting, ridiculous verse which was now
out of fashion, though plays as crude were being
acted at the Rose Theatre by the rival company
of the Admiral's Men under Edward Alleyn.
Falstaff parodies Alleyn's robustious manner in a
tragic part.

my leg: my curtsey.   P. 65 L. 13

O the father . . . countenance: By God, what a straight   P. 65 L. 18
face he keeps!

trustful: trusty; often emended to *tristful:* sad.   P. 65 L. 19

these harlotry players: As the Admiral's men were the   P. 65
only other company acting in London at this time,   LL. 22–23
the parody of their heavy style is obvious. *harlotry:*
worthless.

For though the camomile . . . : Falstaff speaks in a   P. 65 L. 27
parody of the Euphuistic style of Lyly and the
novelists of the 1580s, as antiquated by 1597 as
Macaulay's style is today. This particular simile was
commonly used.

Manningtree: Manningtree in Essex was famous for   P. 67 L. 10
its Whitsun fair when an ox was roasted whole.

vice: the devil in the old Morality plays who was   P. 67 L. 11
armed with a wooden sword and noisily played the
fool.

P. 67 L. 27   *saving your reverence:* often contracted to 'sir-reverence', a phrase apologising for an improper remark.

P. 68 L. 9   *watch:* Before the creation of regular police each parish called on citizens to serve as watchmen. When necessary the Sheriff or Constable could summon their aid.

P. 68 L. 20   *essentially made:* probably a misprint for 'mad', spelt in the manuscript 'madd'. Elizabethan 'd' and 'e' were very similar.

P. 68 L. 23   *deny your major:* a term used in academic arguments. 'I deny your major premise' – the argument by which your conclusion is proved. Falstaff puns also on 'mayor', for mayor and major were pronounced alike.

P. 68 L. 24   *cart:* i.e., which will carry him to his hanging.

P. 69 L. 3   *hue and cry:* the primitive, but often effective, method of apprehending criminals. When a crime was detected everyone turned out to pursue the criminal, and the hue and cry was taken up from parish to parish until the thief was run down, or escaped.

P. 69 L. 11   *Sheriff:* pronounced, and often spelt, 'shrieve'.

P. 70 L. 31   *nativity:* moment of birth.

P. 71 L. 1   *cressets:* stars blazing like beacon fires.

P. 71   *teeming earth . . . wind:* This theory of earthquakes –
LL. 16–18   that they were caused by the expulsion of wind from within the earth – was generally held.

P. 72 L. 2   *read to me:* been my teacher.

P. 72 L. 3   *trace . . . art:* follow me in the difficult practice of magic.

P. 72 L. 4   *hold me pace:* keep up with me.

P. 73 L. 6   *indentures tripartite:* agreements between three parties.

P. 75 LL. 8–9 *profited . . . concealments:* expert in strange mysteries.

P. 77 L. 5   *swilling heavens:* i.e., weeping eyes. Mortimer as a young man in love naturally uses poetical speech.

feeling disputation: a conversation carried on by P. 77 L. 10
feeling, not words.

governed by humours: controlled by your own P. 78 L. 10
whims.

comfit-maker: confectioner, a mild occupation. P. 78 L. 25

sarcenet surety: 'you swear by things as soft as P. 78 L. 28
sarcenet' (fine silk).

Finsbury: Finsbury Fields, a place where citizens P. 78 L. 29
and their wives took a Sunday afternoon walk.

velvet-guards: citizens and their wives in their P. 78 L. 33
Sunday best – peaceful folk.

tailor . . . red-breast teacher: also timid occupations. P. 79 LL. 3–4

out . . . blood: through one of my own children. P. 79 L. 22

affections . . . ancestors: natural desires which fly so P. 80
different a course; i.e., why are you so degenerate LL. 15–16
a member of the family.

common hackney'd: i.e., at every man's call. A *hackney* P. 80 L. 25
is a horse for hire.

loyal to possession: loyal to him who held the throne, P. 80 L. 28
i.e., Richard II.

bavin wits: wits as slight as twigs. P. 81 L. 13

stand . . . comparative: endure the attacks of every P. 81
boy who cared to make jokes at his expense. LL. 18–19

vile participation: mixing with vile society. P. 82 L. 6

in debt to years, than thou: See note on P. 24, L. 28. P. 82 L. 23

fill the mouth . . . up: to make up the number of those P. 83 L. 3
who defy us.

start of spleen: impulsive bad temper. P. 83 L. 12

fallen away: grown thin. P. 85 L. 6

brewer's horse: In Shakespeare's time, brewers' horses P. 85 L. 13
were notorious for their lean poor condition.

Admiral: the admiral's ship, which at night was P. 85 L. 30
illuminated with a lantern so that the rest of the ships
in the squadron could follow.

death's-head: a skull, as a reminder that all men P. 86 L. 5
are mortal.

P. 86 L. 7   *Dives:* the rich man in the parable of Dives and Lazarus; Luke 10: 19–31.

P. 86 L. 10   *by ... Angel:* a parody of one of the more striking lines in Chapman's *Blind Beggar of Alexandria,* a recent success of the rival company, the Admiral's Men.

P. 86 L. 21   *salamander:* this kind of lizard was supposed to like fire.

P. 87 L. 21   *make a younker:* treat me like a boy.

P. 87 L. 25   *ring was copper:* Copper-gilt was the cheapest kind of imitation gold.

P. 87 L. 26   *sneak-cup:* a low thief who stole cups from taverns.

P. 87 L. 33   *Newgate fashion:* like prisoners marching in pairs.

P. 88 L. 24   *drawn fox:* a fox chased into the open, and so cunning.

P. 88 L. 24   *Maid Marian ... to thee:* Maid Marian, the woman in Robin Hood's gang, was a character in a morris-dance, lumpish and awkward, and played by a man. The wife of the deputy of the ward was likely to give herself airs of dignity. So Falstaff means 'You are more awkward than Maid Marian contrasted with a most stately matron'.

P. 90 L. 28   *unwash'd hands:* without waiting to wash your hands.

P. 91 L. 24   *season's stamp: lit.,* of this year's minting, born in these times.

P. 91 L. 25   *general current:* widely accepted.

P. 91 L. 24   *by deputation:* deputy, i.e. he could not send any one else.

P. 93 L. 3   *his present want:* lack of him at the present time.

P. 93 L. 9   *bottom ... soul of hope:* end and last hope.

P. 93 L. 27   *fearful faction:* rebellion full of fear.

P. 94 LL. 26–7   *daff'd ... pass:* i.e., waved the world aside, and let it go: *bit it pass:* i.e., 'without caring a damn'.

P. 94 L. 29   *all plum'd ... bath'd:* These lines are much annotated. As they stand, the meaning is 'All wearing plumes like ostriches that flap the wings (*baited*) like eagles that have just bathed'. The comparison seems hardly apt. Either a line has been omitted after *wind* or *with* is a misprint of some such verb as 'wing'.

feathered Mercury: Mercury, messenger of the gods, P. 95 L. 4 is represented with wing'd sandals.

Sutton Cophill: (in other texts Col'fil') Sutton Cold- P. 96 L. 10 field in Warwickshire.

answer the coinage: guarantee the payment. P. 96 L. 15

If I be not ashamed . . . every hedge: Falstaff's methods P. 96 L. 19– of lining his own pocket and of collecting recruits P. 97 L. 23 were common during the war period. The Counties were responsible for providing men when called upon, but they usually sent their worst, glad to be rid of rogues. Thus in February 1593 the officers appointed to inspect levies reported that 'of 50 men sent by the County of Bedford 14 were unable and insufficient, and most of them very evilly apparelled, their coats of very bad cloth and unlined. Of the 50 men levied in the County of Cambridge but 49 had arrived in London, one having run away, and of the rest ten were insufficient; most of them are ill and nakedly apparelled, wanting doublets, hose, stockings, shirts and shoes, their cassocks also of very bad cloth and unlined'. [*An Elizabethan Journal,* p. 195.]

caliver: a light musket, one of the weapons of the P. 96 L. 27 infantry.

Ancients: ensigns, the junior officer in a company. P. 96 L. 31

Lazarus in the painted cloth: in houses and inns, P. 97 L. 1 which could not afford tapestry, cloths painted with scenes, usually from Scripture, were hung on the walls.

cankers . . . world: maggots that breed in peace. P. 97 LL. 5–6

gibbets . . . bodies: The bodies of executed felons were P. 97 often hung up in iron cages near the scene of the LL. 12–13 crime till they rotted away.

had . . . prison: This was a regular practice, officially P. 97 L.17 recognized

a. 89 L. 8   *toss:* to toss on a pike.

P. 98 L. 16   *three fingers:* the thickness of three fingers.

P. 99 L. 2   *looks . . . supply:* is he not still intent all his troops?

P. 99 L. 11   *well respected:* well- considered – not foolhardy.

P. 99 L. 19   *great leading:* experienced generalship.

P. 100 L. 33   *sue his livery:* prove his title as heir. See *Richard II*, II. 1. 203; II. 3. 129.

P. 101 L. 6   *cap and knee:* i.e. with outward signs of respect.

P. 101 L. 26   *was personal:* went in person.

P. 102 L. 9   *head of safety:* safety in rebellion.

P. 102   *pry Into his title:* to examine closely his right to the
LL. 9–10 throne.

P. 102 L. 24   *Sir Michael:* (called 'Sir Mighell' in the first quarto) He has not been identified, but presumably is a priest or follower in the Archbishop's household.

P. 103 L. 3   *bide the touch:* be put to the test.

P. 103 L. 10   *rated sinew:* valued ally.

P. 103 L. 23   *special head:* best soldiers.

P. 104 L. 9   *Falstaff:* It is worth noting that Shakespeare places Falstaff in immediate attendance on the King.

P. 104 L. 27   *churlish knot:* knot which ties men together for a brutal purpose.

P. 104 L. 28   *obedient orb:* sphere of obedience, like a planet following its natural course.

P. 104 L. 30   *exhal'd meteor:* a meteor formed from vapours drawn up by the sun.

P. 105 L. 1   *broached mischief:* mischief set abroach, *lit.*, tapped like a cask.

P. 105 L. 24   *new-fall'n right:* i.e. the Dukedom to which he succeeded at the death of old John of Gaunt, his father.

P. 106 L. 4   *general sway:* supreme rule.

P. 107 L. 25   *wait on us:* are our ministers.

P. 108   *honour pricks me on . . . prick me off:* Either Shakes-
LL. 13–14 peare invented this jest or else he was using a current phrase. It turns up again in a letter written by Toby Matthew in September 1598, describing how various

young soldiers have gone to the Low Countries:
'honour pricks them on, and the world thinks that
honour will quickly prick them off again.' *Prick on:*
spur forward. *Prick off:* tick off on a list.

scutcheon: a coat of arms, painted on a buckram P. 108 L. 23
banner or a large board, and displayed at the funerals
of gentlemen. Many still survive in old churches.

adopted . . . privilege: i.e. his nickname 'Hotspur' P. 109 L. 17
will be his excuse.

live upon my head: I shall be held responsible. P. 109 L. 18

Deliver up . . . Westmoreland: Westmoreland has P. 109 L. 29
been hostage for the safe return of Worcester.

liberty: Some editors unnecessarily alter to 'liber- P. 111 L. 9
tine'; but Shakespeare often uses the abstract word
for the concrete.

dial's point: hour hand of a clock. P. 111 L. 22

temper: (of steel) hardness. P. 111 L. 33

esperance Percy: The war cry of the Percies: see P. 112 L. 3
P. 52 L. 5.

sembably furnished: wearing armour similarly marked. P. 113 L. 4

Ah fool, go with: sometimes emended to 'A fool go P. 113 L. 5
with thy soul', a picturesque way of saying, 'you
 are a fool'.

shot-free: without paying the 'shot' – the cost of my P. 113 L. 16
drinks.

I have led my ragamuffins . . . left alive: Falstaff's P. 113
motives, as always, are low. Until found out at a LL. 21–2
muster, he will continue to draw and pocket the
pay of his slain worthies. Many Elizabethan captains
were sorry ruffians, and this kind of abuse was too
common.

Turk Gregory: Pope Gregory VII (died 1085) who P. 113 L. 33
before his elevation was the monk Hildebrand; he
had a reputation for ferocity.

pierce: pronounced 'perse'. According to tradition P. 114 L. 14
(romantic but unreliable) the Percy name came from
'pierce-eye'. When Malcolm III, King of Scotland,
invaded England and demanded the surrender of

Alnwick Castle from Robert de Mowbray, Mow-bray hung the keys on a spear and when the King was about to take them, he pierced him through the eyes. Thereafter the family took the name of Percy.

P. 115 L. 22   *Hydra's heads:* Hydra was a nine-headed monster slain, with some difficulty, by Hercules, for, as soon as he had hacked off one head, two more appeared.

P. 116 L. 26   *make up:* go up to the front line.

P. 117 L. 23   *But thought's . . . stop:* 'yet thinking lasts only during life, and life is at the mercy of time: and time itself will end.'

P. 118 L. 24   *Embowell'd:* at the end of the hunt the dead deer were disembowelled.

P. 119   *bravely . . . sword:* behaved bravely in your first
LL. 11–13 battle.

GLOSSARY

Amamon: the name of a fiend
angel: a coin worth 10s.
antic: a clown
apple John: a wrinkled apple
apprehension: notion, perception
approve: put to the proof
arbitrement: judgement
arras: hangings, curtains
articulate: tabulate

balk'd: laid out in rows
band: bond
bastard: a sweet Spanish wine
bastinado: a thrashing with a stick
battle: army
beard: dare
beaver: front part of the helmet
beldam: grandmother
berlady, birlady: by our Lady
blue-caps: Scots
bolters: sieves for sifting flour
bolting hutch: flour bin
bombard: large leather jug
book: agreement
bootless: vain
boots: booty
bots: worms
bottom: valley
brach: bitch
brief: letter
Bristow: Bristol
brook: endure
bumbast: cotton padding

caddis-garter: worsted garter

canker: (1) wild-rose, (2) maggot
canstick: candlestick
cantle: piece, slice
capitulate: draw up the heads of an agreement, plot
carbonado: piece of meat slashed for broiling
carded: lit., mixed with base liquor
cates: delicacies
chamber-lie: urine
chandler: candle merchant
charge: (1) possessions, (2) expenditure
chewet: jackdaw
choler: wrath
christen: christian
chuffs: churls
cital: recital
clipp'd: enclosed
colt: cheat
commodity: consignment
community: a common thing
comparative: wit
compass: limit
confound: spend
contagious: poisonous
contracted: betrothed
corrivals: partners
cousin: used of any relation by blood
cozening: cheating
cranking: winding
cressets: beacon lights, large torches

crop ear: with short ears
crossing: opposition
cuisses: thigh pieces
curst: peevish

daff'd: thrust aside
dangerous: threatening
denier: small copper coin worth one-tenth of a penny
deputation: by deputy
division: cunning music
dog: follow like a dog
dowals: cheap coarse linen
draff: pigwash
drawer: barman, potboy

Ebrew: Hebrew
ell: 45 inches
emboss'd: swollen
enfeoff'd: pledged as a pawn, held as hostage
engross: buy up wholesale
envy: malice
estimation: reputation
exact: entire
expedition: progress, haste

factor: agent
fadom-line: fathom line
fantasy: imagination, hallucination
fat: stuffy
favour: (1) face, feature, (2) scarf
flesh'd: blooded
flowrets: little flowers
forswearing: swearing falsely
franklin: rick farmer
front: forehead
frontiers: defences
fubb'd: cheated

furnish'd: equipped

gage: pledge, engage
griffin: a fabulous beast, half lion, half eagle

hair: quality, grain
half fac'd: insincere
harlotry: silly girl
harness: armour
head: armed forces
hest: command, action
hind: (1) female deer, (2) servant, slave
hold in: say nothing
holy day: pretty
holland: fine linen
holp: helped
humorous: touchy, whimsical
humour: whim, idiosyncrasy

ignis fatuus: will o' the wisp
immask: conceal as with a mask
impressed: conscripted
incursions: raids
induction: beginning
innovation: revolution
irregular: unruly

jade: second-rate horse
jordan: chamber-pot
journey bated: road weary

land-rakers: footpads
lards: drips fat on
leaping-house: brothel
lieve: soon
liking: good condition
line: support
links: small torches

liquor'd: greased to keep out water

list: edge

loaden: laden

loggerheads: blockheads

main: stroke

makes: comes to

mammets: dolls

manage: horsemanship

mark: 13s. 4d.

medecines: love-philtres

micher: truant

minion: darling

misconstrued: misunderstood

misprision: misunderstanding

misquote: misinterpret

mo: more

moiety: share

moldwarp: mole

nice: exact

night-tripping: coming steathily by night

noted: well known

not pated: close cropped

ob: obol, halfpenny

off'ring side: the side taking the offensive

opinion: (1) the common will, (2) arrogance, conceit

orb: sphere course

ought: owed

owe: own

palisado: palisade, defence work of stone

paraquito: parrot

parcel: particular

parmaceti: spermaceti

part: party

passion: agitation

patience: endurance

Pegasus: the winged horse of the hero Perseus

personal: in person

Phoebus: the sun god

pick thanks: talebearers

pismires: ants

popinjay: parrot

portly: prosperous-looking

post: official messenger

post: (*vb*): ride fast

poulter: poulterer

power: army, forces

presently: immediately

prune: preen

puke-stockinged: with dark grey stockings

pupil age: boyhood

purchase: thieves' slang for 'plunder'

quit: pay for

rabbit-sucker: young rabbit

razes: roots

reprisal: prize of war

reversion: portion yet to come

sanguine: suffering from the sanguine humour

semblably: in like manner

serve: i.e., as an apprentice

seven stars: the Pleiades

soused: picked

sovereignest: most efficacious

spleen: vicious temper

squire: rule, measure

starting-hole: bolt hole

still: always

stockfish: dried salt fish
stomach: appetite
stronds: strands
sullen: dull
summer house: country house
swathling: swaddling

task'd: taxed
tasking: challenge
tender: regard
totter'd: ragged
Trojan: gay lad
tun: barrel
twelve score: i.e., paces of five feet

underskinker: under-drawer
unsorted: ill-sorted
uphold: put up with

vassal: slave
vizards: masks

wild of Kent: weald of Kent
withers: shoulders

yet: still

'Zblood: by God's (Christ's) blood
'Zounds: by God's (Christ's) wounds

MORE ABOUT PENGUINS

Penguin Book News, which appears every month, contains details of all the new books issued by Penguins as they are published. From time to time it is supplemented by *Penguins in Print*, which is a complete list of all books published by Penguins which are in print. (There are nearly three thousand of these.)

A specimen copy of *Penguin Book News* will be sent to you free on request, and you can become a subscriber for the price of the postage – 3s for a year's issues (including the complete lists). Just write to Dept EP, Penguin Books Ltd, Harmondsworth, Middlesex, enclosing a cheque or postal order, and your name will be added to the mailing list.

Another book published by Penguins is described overleaf.

Note: *Penguin Book News* and *Penguins in Print* are not available in the U.S.A. or Canada

INTRODUCING SHAKESPEARE

a new and revised edition

G. B. Harrison

This new edition of *Introducing Shakespeare* has been completely revised and expanded, and in particular a new chapter has been added on the age of Shakespeare, together with a set of new line drawings by Walter Hodges, showing the evolution of the Elizabethan playhouse, and many new plates.

Introducing Shakespeare was specially written for Pelicans and serves as a general introduction to the Penguin Shakespeare (of which Dr Harrison is the editor). It deals first and foremost with the legend and then with the life (so tantalizingly ill-recorded) of Shakespeare. The author shows the methods, discoveries, and conclusions of modern inquiry. He explores the Elizabethan playhouse and examines the effect of its complicated structure on the playwright's approach to his theme. There is a chapter on Shakespeare's company, the Lord Chamberlain's men, and it is in this section that the human context of the poet's life is most strongly felt, as we read of rival companies, trade wars, literary piracy, the shutting of the playhouses for fear of the plague, the dangerous performance of Richard II at the time of Essex's rising, and finally the burning down of the Globe theatre. He traces the development of Shakespeare's style, and in a final chapter, Dr Harrison discusses the problems of editing Shakespeare for the modern reader.